D0173567

THE EVERYTHING
GROOM BOOK

Dear Reader,

Whether you're about to ask her to marry you, or whether you've already put the ring on her finger, congratulations are in order. You've found The One and you're moving into an exciting and hectic time in your life: wedding planning.

Your bride-to-be is probably going to look for (and expect) your opinion on just about everything—especially if the two of you are paying for the wedding yourselves. This book will take you through just about every wedding issue that you'll face—and there may be some that will take you completely by surprise.

When my husband and I got married in the early 1990s, grooms weren't expected—or even welcome, really—to take part in the planning. In the last ten years, there has been a dramatic change in how grooms approach their weddings. Many men are very involved nowadays—but the availability of Groom Planners doesn't quite match that of Bridal Planners. I hope this book will be a great help to you as you plan your wedding—from popping the initial question through mapping out the honeymoon.

Best wishes,

Shelly Hagen

The EVERYTHING Series

These handy, accessible books give you all you need to tackle a difficult project, gain a new hobby, or even brush up on something you learned back in school but have since forgotten. You can read from cover to cover or just pick out information from our four useful boxes.

 Alerts: Urgent warnings

 Essentials: Quick handy tips

 Facts: Important snippets of information

 Questions: Answers to common questions

When you're done reading, you can finally say you know **EVERYTHING**®!

PUBLISHER Karen Cooper

DIRECTOR OF ACQUISITIONS AND INNOVATION Paula Munier

MANAGING EDITOR, EVERYTHING® SERIES Lisa Laing

COPY CHIEF Casey Ebert

ACQUISITIONS EDITOR Katrina Schroeder

DEVELOPMENT EDITOR Elizabeth Kassab

EDITORIAL ASSISTANT Hillary Thompson

EVERYTHING® SERIES COVER DESIGNER Erin Alexander

LAYOUT DESIGNERS Colleen Cunningham, Elisabeth Lariviere, Ashley Vierra, Denise Wallace

THE
EVERYTHING®
GROOM
BOOK

A survival guide for men!

Shelly Hagen

adamsmedia
Avon, Massachusetts

For those sensitive, involved, helpful future husbands out there.
Remember that planning the wedding is just the beginning.
The skills you acquire during this process (negotiating,
communicating, budgeting) are your primer for married life.

Published by
Adams Media, a division of F+W Media, Inc.
57 Littlefield Street, Avon, MA 02322. U.S.A.
www.adamsmedia.com

ISBN 10: 1-4405-0359-1
ISBN 13: 978-1-4405-0359-7

Printed in the United States of America.

10 9 8 7 6 5 4 3 2 1

Library of Congress Cataloging-in-Publication Data
is available from the publisher.

This publication is designed to provide accurate and authoritative information with regard to the subject matter covered. It is sold with the understanding that the publisher is not engaged in rendering legal, accounting, or other
professional advice. If legal advice or other expert assistance is required,
the services of a competent professional person should be sought.
—From a *Declaration of Principles* jointly adopted by a Committee of the
American Bar Association and a Committee of Publishers and Associations

Many of the designations used by manufacturers and sellers to distinguish
their product are claimed as trademarks. Where those designations appear
in this book and Adams Media was aware of a trademark claim, the designations have been printed with initial capital letters.

This book is available at quantity discounts for bulk purchases.
For information, please call 1-800-289-0963.

Acknowledgments

A lot of people went out of their way in helping me convey some fairly vital information to the would-be grooms out there. For their assistance, I would like to thank Jennifer Rung, Karyn Shanks, Karen Hill, Mike and Diane Young, Brian Meissner, Chad Ratacjzak, and the other brides and grooms who handed over their stories (whose full names I won't disclose). Thanks to Bethany Brown at Adams and to my agent, Jessica Faust at Bookends, for their insight and help in getting this book off the ground in the first place. And I want to thank my own husband, Mike, who never once brought up the fact (as I sat writing about difficult and emotional brides) that throughout my own wedding planning process, I myself was a Bride from Hell. He's proof positive that any groom can make it through their own fiancée's can't-find-the-right-dress-or-the-right-band meltdown . . . and find happiness on the other side.

THE TOP TEN REASONS YOU SHOULD GET INVOLVED IN PLANNING THE WEDDING . . . NOW

1. Do you really want to eat nouvelle cuisine at your reception?
2. Your girlfriend is planning a fairy-tale-princess-themed wedding . . . and you're Prince Charming (tights and all).
3. You'll appreciate everything your fiancée is going through if you experience some of it firsthand.
4. Your title in your fraternity was "Party-Planning Animal." Share the wealth, man.
5. You don't have to shop for a dress; calling a caterer or two is easy in comparison.
6. Score huge bonus points with the bride just for being interested.
7. You can honestly take credit for a great ceremony and reception.
8. Eliminate the possibility of your girlfriend hiring the "Most Sensitive Band in Town."
9. Is it really fair for your bride to be taking on all of the work?
10. It's fun! (No, really. It is.)

Contents

Introduction

CONGRATULATIONS! You've found the girl you plan to spend the rest of your life with . . . so how *do* you get from here to eternity?

Unfortunately, you may notice that the vast majority of wedding-planning resources are geared primarily toward brides. Many wedding books come packaged in pastel sheaths with bows attached and the words "Bridal Planner" screaming from their covers. (No, no one really expects you to accept these as your Wedding Primers. Even the most expressive man on the planet has his limits.)

The best way to truly appreciate the significance of your wedding is to get involved from the very beginning. Don't just slide in the week before you say, "I do" and give your opinion on the dinner being served at the reception. Go and look at that hall with her before she books it. If it's too small, tell her. If you think it smells kind of weird, say so. Don't wait until you arrive at your reception to voice your concerns. Get in the game early on. Your fiancée really is listening and will love you all the more for it.

Weddings are chock full of details, so be forewarned: You're embarking on a time-consuming venture. Brides have been known to lose their heads while planning their nuptials—but perhaps these particular brides didn't have a partner who was willing to take on some of the responsibility of the wedding arrangements. Helping your bride is going to be your duty for many, many years to come. There's no time like the present to start.

This book is meant to serve as a little guide for the man who has absolutely no idea where to begin this prewedding journey. Women have an unfair advantage in the wedding planning arena, as they routinely dream of their wedding day decades in advance of the actual event. Women pay attention to every minute detail of their friends' and relatives' weddings, and file each item away in one of two separate memory banks: Things I Would Do at My Own Wedding and Things I Would Not Do at My Own Wedding. (You think this is a joke? It's not.) Men tend to do something far less insane at weddings: They attend and enjoy the party. They generally don't spend the evening whispering to their friends about the cheap quality of the table linens.

As you make your first foray into this foreign territory, you may feel as though your fiancée is speaking another language. Think of this book as your translator. It covers everything you need to know about weddings from the most rudimentary responsibilities (e.g., choosing groomsmen, arranging the rehearsal dinner, and behaving at your bachelor party) to the big picture (e.g., preparing the guest list, finding exactly the right spot to say your vows, picking a china pattern). You decide where you fall in the scheme of things—your information is right here.

CHAPTER 1

Please Marry Me!

So this is it. She's The One, and you intend to make it a legal match made in heaven. So where do you start? When should you ask her? How should you ask her? How much should you really spend on a ring—and what *kind* of ring are you going to buy for her? Don't let yourself get overwhelmed by this part. People get married all the time. Remember, *everyone* sets out from Square One. Let's get this show on the road.

Ring Buying 101

Buying an engagement ring sounds like an easy enough task. After all, men do this every day, right? Of course they do. But just because the jewelry shops are full of customers doesn't necessarily mean that any of those customers know what they're doing. Sure, your buddy bought his girlfriend a beautiful ring—but does he have any idea whether or not it's a quality diamond? Before you start your shopping, educate yourself a little and be prepared to do a lot of legwork. Yep, you'd better shop around.

The Basics

First things first: You can't walk into a jewelry store without knowing the first thing about the product you're looking for, or you may end up paying *way* too much for an inferior diamond. Be an informed consumer and know at least the rudimentary facts.

♦ **Carat vs. karat.** One refers to the purity of a precious metal; the other refers to the weight of a diamond. Which is which? (Big hint: *Carat* refers to diamond weight, which is a huge factor in the price of the ring you're looking at.)

♦ **Diamond grading.** When a diamond is appraised, it's put through a rigorous examination that includes an evaluation of the color and clarity of the stone—these, in turn, affect its value.

♦ **The four C's of diamonds.** Color, clarity, carat, and cut. Many jewelers will use this all-encompassing phrase

when you're looking at their goods, so you should
know what they're referring to.

♦ **Big stores vs. independent jewelers.** Although the big
stores advertise more, the smaller guys may be able to
work out a better deal with you. After all, they're running their own business, they set their own prices, and
they don't have the overhead that the bigger stores do.

What Does She Want?

If you and your girlfriend have been planning this
engagement (in other words, it's not going to come as a
complete surprise), she probably has some idea of the type
of ring she'd like to have. Many couples go shopping for the
ring together nowadays, so don't feel like you're ruining
anything by asking her if she'd like to browse in some shops
with you. She doesn't have to be there when you make the
final purchase (hence recapturing the element of surprise),
but you can at least get a pretty good idea of what she's
interested in—and you'll be relieved if it's wildly different
from what you were planning on buying for her.

 Alert

If you feel you just *have* to have a ring when you ask her
to marry you and you don't want to include her in the
purchase, *make sure* your jeweler will exchange it in the
event that she prefers something different.

The *shape* of the stone is often very important to women.
Some women have very strong opinions about what type of

cut they prefer, so if your fiancée is looking at a princess cut diamond, but you really like the pear-shaped one . . . give in to her on this. Yes, the ring is a gift from you, but *she'll* be wearing it every day for the rest of her life. She has to feel comfortable with it. (If she thinks that the pear-shaped diamond makes her fingers look fat or misshapen, for example, she's going to think about how great the princess cut would have looked—*every day*.)

Be Observant

In addition, many women have definite preferences as far as precious metals are concerned. Some women love gold and would never wear silver (or vice versa); other women prefer platinum. If you notice that your girlfriend never wears anything but silver, it could well be because she doesn't like the look of gold. Be safe and stick with her partialities on this purchase.

 Essential

No matter how much you decide to spend, make sure you've covered all of your bases before you plunk down your hard-earned cash. This is, after all, a major purchase—and one that you and your girlfriend will live with for all eternity.

Your best bet is to give yourself plenty of time to shop around, compare prices, and do some research. Web sites like *www.adiamondisforever.com* and *www.debeers.com*

will give you a heads-up on what you need to know *before* you leave the house to shop for an engagement ring.

Two Months' Salary? Really?

Somewhere, someone (probably a jeweler with a big mortgage and kids to put through college) came up with this "guideline" for how much you should spend on your fiancée's diamond ring. This figure is likely close to the amount of credit that will be extended to you by any jewelry store. Whether or not you're comfortable spending that much dough is up to you—and your fiancée, to some extent. If the two of you have been discussing buying a home or a car, carefully consider to what extent your finances can support a ring. It's possible that your fiancée would much rather have the house than the ring.

 Fact

Buy her a ring you can reasonably afford. Going into serious debt in order to buy her the absolute best may seem like a good idea right now, but soon enough you're going to want (and need) other things—a house, a car, furniture, and so on.

If you're *wavering* on the issue of a ring, though, keep this in mind: As life progresses (and it will, more quickly than you realize) there will be expense after expense. Now is probably the *best* time to take the plunge and buy a diamond (one that you can afford, that is). It will become less of a financial priority as the years go by and you have a mortgage, car payments, and kids.

In the end, you have to be realistic. *Of course* you love her so much that you want to get her the biggest, best diamond in the city, but slow things down enough to look at the big picture of your *future* finances (i.e., talk yourself out of going into massive debt in order to buy her a massive ring). Take a deep breath and repeat this mantra, "The diamond is not a metaphor for my love." You can show her you love her in a million ways—spending every last dime on a ring (and borrowing against many future dimes) may not be the best way.

Before you walk into a jewelry store, set a spending limit for yourself (based on your income vs. your debt) and stick to it. And be strong in your resolve not to overspend. Tricky jewelers will try to push you over your limit, and they'll use your love for your girlfriend as a weapon against you. ("If you *really* loved her, you'd get her the three-carat ring.") The salespeople in the jewelry shops will be very kind to you. Remember that their main goal is to make a buck. They *will* try to sell you things that you really can't afford, so be on guard and *say no* when you must.

Getting the Timing Right

You know you shouldn't ask her to marry you when her life is in total upheaval. (You *do* know that, don't you?) But should you ask her before she leaves on her year-long transfer to Europe, or after? If you know there's no chance of the two of you tying the knot for at least another two years, should you wait until the right time approaches? What are the benefits and drawbacks to long engagements?

Her House Just Burned Down . . .

She's also been fired, oh, and her dog died, too. Don't ask her to marry you now. The best thing you can do for your girlfriend when her life is falling apart is stick with her through it. Look at puppies with her; help her find work; pick through the ashes of her building with her—but hold on to the ring for now.

Don't spring a proposal on her if her life is in turmoil. A woman in crisis is not in any position to pledge her life to you. She's just trying to get through each day as it comes. Eventually the smoke will clear (no pun intended) and the right time for a proposal will present itself.

Bon Voyage, My Love!

One of you is leaving town, either temporarily or for good. If you weren't thinking about marriage before you reserved the moving van, think twice before asking her to marry you on a whim, as you're pulling away from the curb.

Again, this is a big life upheaval. You're going to miss each other desperately, and it's understandable that you want to have some sort of commitment before you say goodbye. However, a proposal coming *solely* on the heels of an out-of-town transfer is going to seem suspect—as though you need to be engaged simply because of a lack of trust or as a way to hold on to one another.

Benefits of a Long Engagement

If you do decide to have a long engagement (a year or more), you will almost certainly be able to book your first choice of church, reception hall, caterer, and other wedding vendors. And there's more good news: You'll also be giving yourself enough time to save your money so you can pay for your wedding (mostly) in cash, instead of running up big credit card bills or having to scale back on things you really want for your wedding, as you might have to if you were getting married on shorter notice.

 Essential

If one of you is leaving town for good, give each other time to get settled into your new surroundings. When the time is right for a proposal, you'll know, and you'll revel in the happiness of the moment instead of in the trauma of one of you leaving the other.

A long engagement allows you to work out issues in your marriage before you come face-to-face with them. For example, are you going to have children? How many? Will you both continue to work after you have kids, or will one of you stay home? Whose money is going to pay for what? And who's going to be responsible for cooking and cleaning?

Marry Me Now!

Asking her to meet you at the altar a month from now is kind of short notice, but consider the benefits: You won't have to meet with twenty different caterers; you won't have to discuss color schemes and table linens for six months; and you won't have to deal with endless questions from the masses (e.g., "You're *still* engaged? *When's* the big day? That's a long time off, isn't it?")

In addition, quick engagements are incredibly romantic. There's simply not enough time to get fed up with the whole wedding scene, so you're focused only on each other (and not on whether the dress shop used the correct stitching on the bridesmaids' dresses).

Asking Her Dad

Tradition states that you should request her hand in marriage from her father. You scoff at this thought. You barely know the guy. Or maybe he scares you a little. And anyway, this is the twenty-first century. Do you *really* have to sit down with your future father-in-law and express your most heartfelt emotions concerning his daughter? *How* are you supposed to do this, anyway?

Just Do It

If you're leaning hard on the argument that you're not living in a time of arranged marriages, and asking *permission* to marry anyone is ridiculous, you obviously do not want to have any part of chitchatting with her dad. And you have a valid point. After all, she's not exactly her dad's *property*, and it's *her* opinion that matters, anyway.

Consider this, though: Her father loves her, too. He's watched her grow from a little girl to a woman, and he's supported her and loved her all that time. Fathers often have a real soft spot where their daughters are concerned, and they want to know that the man she intends to marry has good intentions, and is forthcoming and honest, corny as it sounds to you right now.

It may seem like an outdated idea, but most fathers who have *any* type of relationship with their daughters will appreciate a future son-in-law who has the fortitude to touch base with them first. (And that doesn't make you look bad, does it?) This includes a father who hasn't lived with his kids for twenty years—so long as he's been involved in his daughter's life after he moved out.

 Essential

Consider this, also: One day you may have a daughter of your own. You'll feel the same way about her, and you'll want to know that the man she intends to marry has courage enough to address the issue with you.

The thing about asking her father is that you're only getting half the job done. A lot of women have been raised in homes headed by their mothers, and while it's tradition (and very nice) to ask for your girlfriend's father's permission . . . it could be interpreted as a sexist move by the woman who was actually in the trenches, rearing this wonderful lady whom you intend to marry—so if you're going to ask for your future father-in-law's permission to marry his daughter, plan on having a chat with her mom, too.

Keep It Simple

There's no need to go off on a poetic tangent, using flowery language and metaphoric images while explaining your intentions (unless you have a dramatic flair for life in general, of course). Put it to your future father-in-law simply: "I've been working for two years at my present company; I'm in a good financial position; I love your daughter very much; I want to spend the rest of my life with her; and I intend to ask her to marry me." (You may also want to include, "I'd like your blessing," since that's essentially what you're asking for.)

You've covered all the big issues here: You're working, so you'll be able to eat after you get married; you've been working for some time, which means you're an ambitious and stable man; and you're ready to commit to marriage. That's all you need to say. Not so hard, right?

Torture Tactics

Be aware that some parents will give you a hard time, either for their own amusement or because they want to see you sweat a little—that way they can tell what you're really made of.

Karen's then-boyfriend, Dennis, had mustered up his courage for this very task. Karen admits that her father can come off seeming "a little scary" and "intimidating," but she is quick to add that he loves to see people—particularly his daughters' boyfriends—squirm. "Dennis' words were: 'I'd like to marry your daughter,'" Karen recalls, barely stifling a laugh, "and my father said, 'I've got three of them. Which one do you want?'"

A lesser man might have been at a loss for words, but Dennis rose to the occasion and replied, "I didn't realize I had a choice. I'll get back to you on that"—which, of course, made Karen's poker-faced father chuckle. Now they're all living happily ever after.

Moms can be just as tough, though, and fiercely protective of their young. Brian experienced this reaction when he sat down for a chat with his future in-laws. He recalls the night he asked his future in-laws for their blessing:

"They were completely stunned, both at the idea of Jeanne getting married and my asking their permission. Their generation threw a lot of tradition out the window for what I'm sure they thought was for good. I think they're surprised to see some of these traditions coming back.

"Jeanne's mom's response was, 'Is this something Jeanne wants?' She apologized later for this, as she thought it must have sounded bad. I recall having respected her having the instinct to ask this question. Personally, I would rake a kid who wants to marry my daughter over the coals."

 **Essential**

Play it safe. Cover your bases. If you're asking her father, ask her mother, too—*especially* in a situation where there's been a divorce. Your intention is to come out smelling like a rose here. Don't flatter one parent at the other's (and your own) expense.

The moral: Be brave, future grooms, and be nimble. Go into this meeting prepared for any eventuality. When all is said and done, no one is going to fault you for having the courtesy and the courage to initiate this conversation with her parents. And unless you and her father come to fisticuffs, you *will* end up proposing in the end.

"I Won't Ask Him"

You're a toughie. You think asking her parents' permission is absolutely ridiculous and you flat-out refuse to do it. No one can force you to follow tradition, and if you won't do it, that's your call. You may luck out: Her parents may like you so much that they won't care, or they may also feel that this is a tradition better left in the past.

However, you might just as likely come off looking bad—if, for example, they really would have preferred to know about the engagement or if they have valid concerns about your impending marriage (e.g., neither you nor your fiancée is working and you plan on living with her parents—except you haven't told them that, either).

In the end, it's a decision you have to make on your own, but raising the topic with her parents before you propose isn't going to hurt your image—while springing a complete surprise on them just might.

How to Ask Her

You bought the ring, you asked her parents, and you've decided the right time to ask her is *now*. You open your mouth to speak . . . and nothing comes out. You've decided the setting isn't right, after all. You'll wait for the perfect moment. When weeks have passed and perfection has yet to present itself, what's a groom to do? Two words: Chill out.

Perfection Is Sometimes Overrated

If you're an idealist and you want everything to be *just so* all the time, you've probably been told that you're too hard on yourself—and on others. While it's completely understandable that you want this moment to be as perfect as possible, you need to realize that "almost perfect" is sometimes as close as you'll get. You can't control certain things. If you plan to ask her to marry you on the terrace of your apartment and a monsoon blows in out of nowhere . . . you can't stop the rain. Move your plans indoors.

 Alert

If you keep putting the proposal off because of factors that are completely out of your control, you may end up delaying your proposal for weeks. She may start to wonder why you're in such a mood all the time.

Obviously, you want certain factors to be in their right places when you propose. If you take the ring box out of your pocket and drop it, don't tell her, "Never mind. We'll try this again later." Remember that the entire point behind this proposal is asking her to spend the rest of her life with you. Everything else (Is the champagne cold enough? Why is that door slightly ajar? Are her fingers a little puffier than usual?) should be of little concern in comparison.

Picking a Spot

If the two of you have a spot that means everything to both of you—or to one of you—your proposal will be doubly romantic if you pop the question there. Were you standing on the bridge in the park when you realized you wanted to spend the rest of your life with her? Did you bump into each other for the first time at the beach, or did you meet while you were both working in a restaurant?

 Fact

Obviously, some locales have a higher romance quotient than others. Use your best judgment in making this decision. You may have met when you sat next to each other at a professional baseball game, but if she was dragged there by her friends and she hates sports as a rule, she won't mind if you propose somewhere else.

Swept Away

Men sometimes get a bad rap, portrayed as being completely unromantic. Nothing could be further from the truth for men on the verge of popping the question, though. When the feeling strikes you, go with it. Don't question it, don't fight it, don't ignore it. Keep in mind, this is one of the biggest things you're going to do in your lifetime, and it's also going to be one of your girlfriend's most vivid memories—something she'll be asked about, something she'll tell your children and grandchildren. The more romantic instinct you have to work with, the better.

You want to plan a weekend in Paris—because it's a kind of crazy, wildly romantic thing to do, and the two of you have always talked about seeing the Eiffel Tower? No time like the present, then—and don't forget to pack the ring.

Of course, you don't need to spend a small fortune to be romantic. Chances are, if you make the smallest effort—to clean yourself up, plan a nice evening, and express your deepest feelings to her before presenting her with the ring—she'll be swept off her feet.

How Not to Ask Her

Your engagement is the first step in the rest of your life with this woman. Take the time to make a plan—even a quick plan—and do it right. You don't want to regret not having done something that you would have, if only you'd thought of it. Your girlfriend doesn't want to hear after the fact that you would have had champagne and roses for her, but it was kind of a lot of trouble and you were tired. Remember: You get one shot at this.

Hit the Showers!

Don't ask her when you're unshaven, kind of stinky, really tired, and generally unkempt. She may be your best friend in the world, and she may see you like this all the time, but this moment is going to be etched in her memory forever. Clean yourself up a little.

While you don't have to think of this as putting yourself on display, maybe you should. What if the tables were turned, and she came to you, in a dirty T-shirt, not having combed her hair all day, looking like she was completely unenthusiastic about the topic at hand—namely, taking you for her lifelong partner?

This is probably an unfair analogy, as many men truly don't *ever* care whether their girlfriend is showered or not. She looks good to you regardless of her cleanliness. Women, however, by and large, *do* care, especially at moments like these. No one is suggesting that you need to have a manicure and buy a tuxedo for the occasion. Just make an effort to be clean and coherent.

You've Been Out Painting the Town . . .

You come home to an irate girlfriend after a wild night on the town, who has told you time and again that she's not going to put up with your rowdy ways anymore. She's ready to call it quits when you hear yourself saying: "I'll change if you marry me!"

Though this might be the most heartfelt statement you've ever made, the situation is just not right. Whether either of you realize or admit it (you both feel that she's completely justified in her threat to walk out—and she probably *is*), this is a proposal made under duress. Things may work out swell; but it's just as possible that you will revert to your old ways and learn to hide the evidence better.

A proposal should be made in a sincere way, and because you want to be with her for the rest of your life— not because you're afraid she's going to walk out on you. (There's a big difference there.) Presenting a proposal in this manner also means that you're promising to amend your errant behavior right away—and now you've got even more on the line if you mess up. Granted, it's the kick in the pants some men (and women, to be fair) need to move forward in their lives; but for others, it's like living life in a pressure cooker.

You've flat-out told her that you're going to change if she marries you—which carries not just an implication, but the promise that you're a new man, starting now. If you mean it, great. Best wishes. If you know you can't live up to this expectation, you need to tell her—and the sooner the better.

Pass the Chips . . . Oh, and Will You Marry Me?

This is going to be one of the most exciting things your girlfriend has ever experienced—the realization that you are, indeed, The One. Even if the two of you have been talking about getting married for months, the proposal is going to knock her for a loop. Treat it like the big deal that it is.

You may be the world's most nonchalant man, taking everything in stride because you despise hoopla. That's fine and well—but you don't have to be a party pooper your entire life. Put your feelings aside for this moment and *act excited* about becoming engaged.

Avoid the casual mention (as you're walking out the door in the morning) that it would be really nice if she would marry you. Don't toss the ring her way as the two of you sit watching the game on TV. Leaving the ring with a note attached to it ("Hey, I was thinking . . . let's get married. P.S. We're out of milk") is completely unacceptable.

This is a milestone in your life. Give it the allotted time, attention, and respect that it deserves. You'll regret it if you don't.

Your girlfriend will fall in love with you all over again when she sees that you—the man with very few emotions—were able to work up a little excitement over the idea of asking her to be your wife.

CHAPTER 2

She Said Yes! Now What?

On to bigger things. You're going to need to let your families in on your engagement pronto, and then you're going to pick a date. You're going to have to come up with a plan for your wedding finances, as well. And once you discover how much money and planning goes into a wedding, you may want to skip it altogether. Maybe the subject of eloping has come up. Is it ever a good idea to run off and get hitched? Keep reading and find out.

Announcing It to the Families

You already asked for her parents' permission. Now do you have to go back and tell them the task is done? Yes, you do. In fact, you need to tell your parents and anyone else who has a stake in your future. You want to send them a postcard telling them you're engaged? You can do better than that.

Together Forever . . . Starting Now

If at all possible, spring this news on the parents together. It'll be a moment they'll never forget, even if they knew it was coming. They're going to be happy, excited, nervous—let both sets of parents get a visual on your euphoria. Let them celebrate and break out the champagne with you. Even though you and your now-fiancée are the ones headed for a huge life change, it's also a big moment for her parents and yours.

Making the Call

But what if you get engaged overseas or across the country and the two of you can't wait until you get back home to announce your news? Calling your parents is perfectly fine—in fact, if you're not going to see them anytime soon, calling may be your only option. Be prepared to speak with her parents and prepare your fiancée to speak with yours.

Do you have kids? Does she? Put the phone down, and prepare yourself for a face-to-face meeting. Ideally, all of you should get together to discuss your impending marriage. Be patient if there are any outbursts (as there may be if the kids had any hope of their parents reconciling, or if you and her kids don't exactly see eye-to-eye on a few things—or vice versa), and be prepared to answer a lot of questions.

 Essential

Play it safe. Cover your bases. If you're asking her father, ask her mother, too—*especially* in a situation where there's been a divorce. Your intention is to come out smelling like a rose here. Don't flatter one parent at the other's (and your own) expense.

Setting the Date

You need one. You can't put off choosing one for too long, because you can't plan your wedding if you don't know when it's going to occur. Chapter 1 discussed the pros and cons of long engagements, and some of those factors (e.g., saving your money over the next two years so that you won't be burdened with extraordinary wedding debt) may come into play here. Your work schedule could be an issue. Or maybe you have a special holiday or a particular season in mind. Whatever the case, you can go no further until this little task is taken care of. Time to get to work.

That's the Day!

Some couples have a certain date in mind, and come hell or high water, they are going to be married on *that* day.

Special dates may include holidays, birthdays, or anniversaries (like the anniversary of the day you met).

 Fact

One perk to choosing a holiday wedding date is that no one will be likely to forget your anniversary. It'll be etched in the minds of your friends and family forever.

If you're leaning toward choosing a multipurpose wedding date, consider some of the potential future cons. Will your anniversary be lost in the shuffle of another important date, for example? Will you wish, year after year, that your anniversary gift wasn't always tied up with your birthday gift? Consider some of these possibilities when selecting a date for your wedding:

♦ Many of your guests may already have other plans—particularly if you've picked a long weekend and/or a major holiday (such as Christmas week).
♦ Your anniversary will never be acknowledged as its own special day.
♦ In the event that things don't go as planned, your birthday will be ruined forever.
♦ You will never, ever get a table (or good service) at your favorite restaurant on Valentine's Day, even if it is your anniversary.

One bride confesses now, ten years after her wedding: "My anniversary is right around Mother's Day—sometimes the dates coincide. We didn't have children when we got married—now that we have small kids, we try to just combine the two things, because we can't really go out for special dinners twice in the same week. Both days usually end up being kind of blah. I think we're going to try alternating years—one year we'll go all out for the anniversary, and the next year I'll get a Mother's Day."

 Fact

If your heart is set on a spring or summer wedding, start planning as early as possible. These are the most popular months for weddings, and unless you're planning on having a backyard ceremony and a barbecue reception, you'll have a heck of a time finding a caterer, a church, a florist, a minister, and a band on less than six months' notice.

Work, Work, Work

Your work schedule is a big consideration when you're choosing a wedding date. Teachers often choose the summer months for their weddings for obvious reasons; accountants avoid the month of April for theirs. These occupations have their definite busy seasons; your work schedule may be less clear. If there's something huge looming on the horizon where you work—you know, for example, that next spring you're going to be sent to work in Asia for three months—try to avoid having your wedding date coincide with a potential work crisis.

If you're on active military duty, plan your wedding cautiously. In this current world climate anything can happen, and you'd hate to throw away all of your money on a wedding that had to be canceled when you were called overseas. It may be wise to either have a small, inexpensive wedding or postpone the wedding altogether until you're discharged.

Good Things to Know

The least expensive time to plan a wedding is in the winter months (between November and January), and the most expensive time of the week is Saturday evening.

If your heart is set on a Saturday (because for many people it's simply the most convenient day to schedule a wedding, especially if you're counting on the company of out-of-town guests) and saving money is a major concern, you can opt for an earlier reception. You won't have to serve as large a meal as you would in the evening, and the savings will be substantial.

Beware: Wedding Emotions Ahead

Unless you've already witnessed a sibling's or a close friend's wedding planning season, you may be surprised to learn that seemingly normal people start to lose it when a wedding is in the works. This can begin immediately after the engagement, so the more aware you are of this potential problem, the better off you'll be. Dealing with your emotional bride and family members is no walk in the park. Be prepared.

Tread Lightly

Your bride is immediately going to start the search for the perfect dress, the one that makes her feel like a princess, the one that makes her look busty *and* thin at the same time. You, on the other hand, will look through the magazines with her (not that she will ever show you *the* dress, because it's bad luck, of course) and you'll think, "These dresses are practically all the same. They've got beads all over them, they're white, and they're really poofy."

You may not understand her frustration at not being able to find the ideal dress. When she comes home crying because she found The Dress, but it costs about $500 more than she wants to spend, you might want to plug your ears. As far as you're concerned, she could show up at the altar wearing overalls and you'd still think she's the most beautiful woman on Earth.

 Essential

Concede the fact that her wedding planning experience and your wedding planning experience are probably very different from each other. And then cut her a little slack and pass her the tissue box if she needs it.

The best thing you can do in this situation is to listen to her. Give her a back rub when she's tense from a day of dress shopping. Make her a cup of tea and hand her some aspirin if she has a headache. Don't initiate a conversation about the ridiculousness of hunting down a dress that seems as elusive as an endangered animal. While your point may be valid, this is not the time to raise the issue. You'll make her cry even more, and she'll also tell you that you couldn't possibly understand how she feels—which you'll acknowledge as being true.

Your bride is living through a highly emotional time in her life; she's actually planning the wedding she's likely been dreaming of for years. That's some serious pressure. Even when men are very involved in the wedding planning process, they tend to be far less prone to tears when they learn that something (the right tux, or a certain band) isn't available for their big day.

Dealing with Family

You and your fiancée are the ones headed to the altar, so why are you going head-to-head with her mother? And yours?

 Alert

You may think it seems easiest to simply get out of the way and let the opinionated kin have his or her way—but chances are you'll regret it. If you care at all about how your wedding proceeds, you need to nip this type of behavior in the bud by reminding your brother, for example, that if he doesn't shape up he can—and will—be replaced.

If there hasn't been a wedding in your family, you may not know that certain family members sometimes become completely unrecognizable during the planning stages. Mothers go berserk; formerly silent fathers put their two cents in; sisters become experts on bridesmaid dresses; and brothers . . . well, most brothers really don't care, but if you ask one to be a groomsman, he may tell you that he is not going to wear a tuxedo. If that's part of the deal, you can forget it.

Do you want to disown your own family and encourage your bride to put herself up for adoption? Hang tight. You're not the only one who has experienced this apparent abduction-and-replacement-with-pod-people of family members. You have one of two options, and each comes with its own set of potential trouble. You can either tell the offending relation to butt out and risk alienating him or her or you can ignore the offender.

Planning the Wedding Finances

So what are we talking here, in terms of money—and how are you going to pay for this, anyway? The answer depends on the type of wedding you're planning: formal, informal, ultra formal?

Before you sit down to hash out just how much you're willing to pay for a band at the reception, put the situation into some sort of perspective: This is a big expense, but it's a one-time thing. You're not going to walk down the aisle with this woman again. If there's something she's always wanted for her wedding (or something you've always imagined for yours), try to slip it into the budget somewhere.

The Cost

When you proposed, you honestly had no idea that this wedding could cost you thousands—nay, *tens* of thousands of dollars. Why should a wedding cake cost 800 bucks? Why should you pay $40 a head for your guests to have a sit-down gourmet meal at your reception? And you just want to see someone *try* to justify the cost of fresh flowers for those centerpieces.

A typical big wedding costs big bucks. Even when you're lucky enough to find a few bargains along the way, everything *else* is going to be expensive. If you want a big wedding—with the church and plenty of guests and a band and your bride in a big white dress—it's going to cost you. There's no way around it.

Wedding Fund?

If the two of you have actually been saving for your wedding since before the proposal, you're probably in fairly good shape. Be careful, though, not to fall into a false sense of financial security, paying too much for a service just because you don't have to pinch pennies. Always look for the best deal, or you will absolutely end up paying too much for something—maybe everything.

To keep your spending in check:

- ◆ Be a little flexible.
- ◆ Give yourself time.
- ◆ Do your own research.

You may not be able to have absolutely everything you both want. If you find that you're running over your budget, perhaps you could substitute a less expensive chicken entrée for prime rib at the reception, for example, or you may have to pare down the guest list.

Start shopping around as early as possible. If there's something you just have to have, you'll be giving yourselves enough time to restructure your budget to include this one particular item, while finding another area to cut back.

Because the wedding industry is huge, you may feel that there's simply too much to look at. That limo guy gave you a price and he assured you that it's the "going rate." Don't take his word for it. He may be counting on your complacency. It will take five minutes for you to make a call to a competitor (or ten minutes to call two other places) and confirm this information for yourself.

Charge It! Or Maybe Not . . .

You have some money saved up, but not nearly enough to pay for the wedding in cash. Should you cut back on the affair, or whip out your plastic? Some couples love the convenience factor of credit; others hate it and opt to pay cash for everything. Using credit doesn't become a problem unless you start charging everything (the dress, the shoes, the flowers, the tuxedos, the rehearsal dinner bill, the honeymoon, etc.).

If you still want to use credit cards for wedding expenses, that's fair enough. You and your bride are adults, and you can certainly spend your future earnings any way you see fit. Try this piece of advice, though: If you do find yourself charging an inordinate amount of wedding expenditures, keep track of it. Buy yourself a little notebook—one that will be unobtrusive sitting in your car door—and also get one for your bride-to-be. Write down every charge as soon as you make it.

Alert

If you say to yourself that you're only getting married once so you might as well do it up big and just charge everything you can't afford, be careful. You'll be more likely to lose track of what you're spending, you're less likely to look for the best deal, and you'll be speechless when those bills start rolling in.

As those tallies start adding up to an exorbitant amount, you may find that you really need to cut back on the spending—and you'll be in a position to take control. If you wait for your monthly statements to roll in, it may be too late to change your mind.

A Little Help Here?

Though the days of the bride's father shelling out big bucks for his daughter's wedding are not quite gone, it's not as commonplace to hear of the bride's family paying for the entire wedding as it was even twenty years ago. Many couples are taking on at least some of the expenses themselves—and rightly so. After all, when both of you are working full-time and making good money, it seems almost silly to expect Mom and Dad to pick up the entire tab for your party.

One caveat about accepting financial assistance: If the monetary gift has certain expectations attached (e.g., her parents want you to have the reception indoors while you and your fiancée really wanted a garden party; your parents expect you to hire that jazz band they love instead of snaring your disc jockey pal) think twice before cashing that "gift" check. From here, your wedding will be in peril of becoming an event you didn't plan—and one you really aren't happy about.

 Fact

If her parents—or your parents—want to chip in and help, great. As long as you and your bride are both comfortable accepting the donation, there's no reason to balk at the idea. If one of you is completely uneasy about accepting this money, however, turn down the offer graciously.

Planners and Consultants

Your bride told you she's thinking that the two of you will need to hire a wedding planner. You laughed out loud and told her she's silly. There's nothing to planning a wedding, you told her. You call the florist, you call the priest, and you show up some Saturday in June. That's all the planning you need . . . right? In a perfect world, maybe.

What Do They Do?

A bridal planner and a wedding consultant essentially perform the same duties. Either will guide your bride (and you, too) through the planning process—as little or as much as you need or want. The benefit to hiring a planner is that she (or he) is already knee-deep in the industry—she knows which vendors are reputable, and which aren't, she knows when to book which service, and she'll know how to make your ideas happen. She already has a lot of contacts out there.

 Alert

If your bride is juggling work, home, and a wedding, she may fall victim to what is referred to in some sectors as a Bridal Meltdown. You will not recognize this woman, but you will know you want be be far, far away from her until she's finished stressing over the wedding.

You're thinking, "Brides have planned weddings for hundreds of years without paying someone else to do it for them. My fiancée has her mom and her friends to help her." (You're so practical.)

True, weddings *have* been planned by brides for centuries —but you're leaving something out of the equation. Your bride probably works full-time. If you add in all the work she brings home and the extra hours at the office, she technically works more than forty hours a week, and she may be on overload right at this moment. Throw a wedding into the mix, and there's no telling what will happen to her emotional state.

What Should You Ask Her?

You'll schedule an initial interview with a bridal consultant. Some topics you'll want to touch base on:

- ♦ How much she charges.
- ♦ How many clients she has at once.
- ♦ What kind of contingency plans she has for emergencies.
- ♦ What kind of budget you've got to work with.

Get the cost issue out in the open right away. Many planners offer different "packages," which means you'll pay for his or her level of involvement in your wedding. If you just want some advice on wedding etiquette, she may offer this as a service; however, if you're looking for someone to dive in and plan your big day—and/or commit to being with your bride from sunrise to sunset on that day—you'll pay considerably more.

 Fact

Your bride will probably have a dozen other questions during this interview, but these will get *you* into the conversation, and give you an idea of what this consultant is going to do for you. You may walk out of that office wondering how you ever thought you could plan this wedding on your own.

Determining her number of clients will give you an idea of your planner's experience, of course, but it will also give you an idea of what kind of attention you can expect from her. If she's booked eight weddings during the same month as yours, she's probably taking on too much, and someone is going to get the shaft.

Contingency plans are a must. What if you're hiring her to be in attendance, running your wedding day, and she comes down with the flu that weekend? Does she have an assistant? Will there be any type of price adjustment?

Finally, giving her a ballpark figure of how much you're looking to spend on the wedding is a great way to determine her ability to work with your budget. Really creative planners can work with any financial plan.

The Pros and Cons of Eloping

Sometimes, engaged couples find that there's something about the big wedding and all that leads up to it that just doesn't sit well with them. It could be the expense, the long wait for the first opening in the reception hall's calendar, the family feuding that sometimes erupts during the planning stages, or a dozen other things. Before the two of you hop the next flight out of town, carefully weigh the pros and cons of taking a powder.

The Advantages

There's a definite upside to leaving all the planning behind and getting on with your life. Consider these things:

Cost

Generally speaking, eloping tends to be a lot less expensive than throwing the huge church-ceremony-and-reception-for-two-hundred shindig. Even if you go all out when you elope and stay in the best hotel, eat gourmet meals, and go for all the bells and whistles in the wedding chapel, you will probably spend far less than you would on a traditional wedding.

Escaping the Family

Your family doesn't like your bride, or maybe her family doesn't like you. Why put yourselves through months of torture, listening to your respective relations trying to convince you that you're marrying the wrong person? Once you're married, you're married. They'll either accept it or they won't, but once you come home married, they'll realize you're committed to your spouse, which is a strong statement.

Timing

Some couples either don't have time to waste (if one of you is leaving town on a job assignment, for example), or simply find it ridiculous to wait around for a random Saturday two years from now, when the *right* caterer is available to feed your guests.

Romance

Eloping ratchets the romance factor way up. You're striking while the iron is hot. You can't live one more day without being married. Your bride will be the envy of her friends, having chosen a guy like you who just *had* to marry her.

No Gawkers

Escaping your immediate family is one thing. If you or your bride is completely uncomfortable being the center of attention, your big wedding could turn out to be nothing short of agony. It doesn't make sense for either of you to be uncomfortable (kissing and greeting all of those strangers/guests; doing the Hokey Pokey; posing for picture after picture after picture) on one of the most important days in your lives together. If either of you sense this will be a problem, start packing.

No Stress

Do a side-by-side comparison of the big wedding vs. eloping. You'll spend months (maybe years) planning the big wedding; you'll shell out big bucks; you'll inevitably fight with someone over the guest list; and by the time the whole thing rolls around, you may feel as though you've been through the wringer. Conversely, eloping entails very little planning; far less cash; and dealing with your family only after your marriage.

Eloping is sounding pretty good at this point? Don't pull out those suitcases yet. You've only considered half of the information on the topic. Keep reading.

The Disadvantages

So . . . you're sold on the idea of eloping? Not so fast. There may be a few reasons to stick around and do things the traditional way.

Your Bride's Dreams

If she's always dreamed of being Princess for a Day, of wearing the big white dress, of having twelve bridesmaids, chances are you're not going to talk her out of it. Women can be very connected to their wedding fantasies, and attempting to talk her into eloping might be like trying to pry that engagement ring off of her finger. Her fantasy, like the ring, is there—and it's not going anywhere. In fact, eloping might result in a lifetime of her telling her friends, "I never had the wedding I really wanted . . . "

Your Own Dreams

Men are often reluctant to admit that they've been thinking about their wedding day since way before they met The One. You might have certain ideas and dreams about a big wedding day (you know which of your friends will be standing up in the church with you; you know the perfect band for the reception; and you're thinking about renting a convertible for the big getaway at the end of the night). Remember: You only get to marry this girl—and be the groom—this one time. If it's a big deal to you to have a big wedding, say so.

Family

Difficult as they can be to deal with, sometimes it's for the best to let your families attend your wedding. If eloping would set you and your bride up for a decade of hard feelings and accusations (her family will think that you "kidnapped" your fiancée; or your family will say that your fiancée "trapped" you), then it may be best to stick things out and get married where both families can see that there was no coercion involved.

Guilt

As much as the two of you want to get away from every stress of planning the big wedding, guilt may creep down the aisle with you, especially if either of you are reluctant to get married on the sly, without the family present. Eloping should be about fun and romance. Make sure tears aren't going to be part of the trip.

The Aftermath

Couples who elope are sometimes forced to face intense scrutiny—not just from family members, but from friends, coworkers, neighbors—anyone who's bold enough to question your marriage. Is your bride pregnant? Does your mother hate your bride? Did your bride's family threaten to boycott a big wedding because they hate you? If you're thick-skinned, this will be no big deal to you. If you're not, it will.

As easy as it seems, eloping *isn't* always easy. An in-depth analysis of your true feelings on the big wedding, along with your predictions of your family's reactions, may be in order before you book your flight out of town.

CHAPTER 3

Engagement Duties

If you've decided against eloping and you're going to stick around for your engagement season, you're going to be busy, busy, busy. You may find yourself one of the guests of honor at an engagement party; you'll formally announce your good news in print; and you may find that this wedding is driving you and your bride to endless discussions on who is and who isn't getting their way. This chapter offers a look at these engagement season issues, including an overview of premarital counseling.

Party!

Engagements are obviously cause for celebration. You and your fiancée are looking forward to a bright, happy future—and the feeling is contagious. Your families are thrilled for the two of you, and someone may raise the issue of hosting an engagement party. (The issue of the bachelor party—which may be more to your liking—will be addressed later in Chapter 9.)

You might think that this sounds like a very formal, upper-crust way to celebrate impending nuptials. This isn't necessarily true. An engagement party is simply a time for your family and friends to come together and toast you and your bride-to-be.

If you've never been to such an event, you might not know what to expect. The truth is, an engagement party in this era can take any form, so if you're agonizing over what to wear, for example, your best bet is to check with your host. He or she will tell you if this is a formal or a casual event . . . and you can take it from there.

Who's Hosting?

Traditionally, the parents of the bride have the option of hosting the first wedding-season party. Of course, this is the twenty-first century, so all bets are off as far as tradition is concerned. *Anyone* can host an engagement party for you.

Whoever is hosting should pick up the tab for the party. Although couples these days are by and large paying for their own weddings, your engagement party is different. This is an event to honor your impending nuptials. You and your bride-to-be are *guests* of the host (assuming the two of you aren't the hosts), and as such, you should not be expected to pay for the band or the food or the wine.

Attire and Guests

An engagement party in this day and age can range anywhere from a formal evening in an upscale restaurant to a clambake at the shore to a luncheon in someone's home—and the setting may or may not influence the size of the guest list (more on this in a bit). More and more people are eschewing tradition in favor of what's easiest (and most economical), and that often means moving a party's location to a place that suits your host's budget.

 **Question**

Can the bride and groom throw a party for themselves?
Traditionally speaking, you shouldn't throw a party to honor yourselves—but it's a safe bet the Etiquette Police won't break things up if you decide to anyway.

While comfort may be an issue for you (you wear jeans every day, so why *can't* you wear them to a formal party?), it's also important for you to respect what your host is doing for you. It won't kill you to wear something a little nicer or a little more formal than what you normally wear, if the location dictates that you should.

Once your host has chosen the location, you may be asked to help with the guest list. Some tips:

♦ **Work with your host.** If your future mother-in-law is asking you for a list of your closest friends and family (which probably means she's looking to keep this party on the small side), don't hand her what amounts to a local phone directory.

♦ **Look to the future.** You should only be inviting guests who will make it onto your final draft of the wedding guest list. To invite them to your engagement party and exclude them from the big day is in incredibly bad taste.

♦ **Gifts are not guests.** If you're including Aunt Marguerite, whom you haven't seen in years, to this small soiree only because she's renown for her gift-giving, cheese it. She'll see right through your ploy. Invite her to the wedding instead.

⊛ Essential

Dress accordingly. Don't wear jeans to the country club (because you really wanted a low-key party); don't wear your new dress pants to the beach (because you really wanted something much more upscale). You'll feel out of place, and what's worse, you'll stick out like a sore thumb, leaving the other guests to question your fashion choices.

"Presents? For *Me*?"

Traditionally speaking, gifts are not given at engagement parties. And anyway, your friends and family may or may not be familiar with engagement party protocol. You shouldn't *ever* expect a gift for any occasion (and yes, this includes your wedding), so if a guest does bring you a little something, be grateful. This is not something you are entitled to just because you popped the question.

 Fact

If socializing ranks right up there with taking a bath in battery acid as far as you're concerned, consider this party a practice run for your wedding, which will be at least as large as (and perhaps larger than) this celebration. There are some things in life that you just have to do. Small talk is one of those things, at least in this situation.

If a guest brings a gift that you and your bride just hate, pretend you love it. You may both despise phoniness and both of you may go out of your way to be brutally honest with people no matter what the situation, but you need to curtail that instinct until after your wedding. Learn the art of saying, "Thank you so much—we love it!" It goes a long way toward cementing your reputation as decent human beings.

Your Duties

Normally, the host of a party carries the weight on his or her shoulders for the entire evening. The guests of honor are not entirely off the hook, however. At your engagement party, you will be expected to be sociable, pleasant, and helpful. You will not be expected to walk around with a tray offering appetizers and champagne to the other guests, but you should speak to everyone in attendance; you should put on a cheery face; and you should, from time to time, ask your host if you can help with anything.

You hate making conversation with near-strangers, you say? The upside of undertaking the chore of chitchatting: You'll win admirers from both sides of the family, and your bride will recognize that you made an all-out effort for the occasion. That will mean a lot to her.

"We're Getting Married, World!"

After you ask her for her hand in marriage, and after you've alerted her family to this fact, you're probably going to want to announce your good fortune to the world. You'll find yourself looking at the engagement pictures in the newspaper, posing in the mirror, and perhaps dreading the actual photo session all at once. Like everything else Wedding, you get one shot at this with this woman. Do it right.

The Picture

The engagement picture is very important to your bride. This bears repeating: The picture that will go in the newspaper announcing your future together is *incredibly* important to your bride. This goes along with her entire wedding fantasy—the one she's been putting together since she was seven. She's got the perfect guy, and she wants everyone to know it. She wants you to look the part, Mister.

Don't take this lightly. If there was ever a time you were going to buy a new sports coat, this may be it. Don't try out that funky, slightly crazy haircut just yet; consider removing the earring from your eyebrow (unless she likes it, of course); don't agree to play tackle football with your buddies in the hours preceding your photo session.

Why do you need to look your best? Aside from the obvious reason that it's a formal picture of the two of you, it's also your first foray into part of her world. Your bride-to-be's long lost friends (and beaux) will probably be seeing you for the first time when this picture hits the newspaper.

Moreover, this picture will be around *forever*. Your mother will buy multiple copies of the newspaper on the day you and your bride-to-be are making your appearance; this picture will be on her refrigerator for years. Your grandmother will send this picture to everyone she knows. Someone will inevitably frame it for you.

 Alert

You don't want to regret looking—in print—like something the cat dragged in, and your fiancée doesn't want to deal with that possibility—or reality—either. That's not part of the wedding fantasy.

The Announcement

A funny thing happens to some couples when they start writing their engagement and/or wedding announcements for their local newspaper—they realize apparently no one at their local paper regularly checks the facts of these articles. No, the person at the Society Page Desk trusts that these young men and women are one hundred percent truthful. Suddenly, the bride, who is still in college, is the CEO of a phony corporation, and *you* have been traveling the world for several years, helping those less fortunate than you (funny how you've managed to make an appearance at the guys' weekly poker game).

So what's wrong with fudging the announcement a little, you ask? No harm done, right? Um . . . wrong. While *truly* outrageous claims may actually prompt a newspaper employee to check into the facts of your life, embellishing your accomplishments even slightly in an engagement announcement is, as a rule, a bad idea. Stick to what you've actually accomplished—not to what you *might* achieve in the future.

First of all, anyone who actually knows you is going to know that you've lied. Secondly, you'll have to keep up the lying at your wedding, because many of your guests will have read your announcement and will assume that you were being absolutely truthful. (Ask anyone who's ever told a whopper how difficult—and uncomfortable—it is to keep up with the lie.) Thirdly, it doesn't speak well for you on the whole.

You're young. No one expects you to own a multimillion dollar company at the age of twenty-five (or thirty, for that matter). You've got your entire life ahead of you to conquer the world. Be honest about what you've done thus far.

If you're worried you haven't done *enough*, realize that you're going to come off looking far worse than you ever could have imagined when everyone realizes you fibbed in a huge way. Seven-year-olds can get away with telling fictitious stories; adults can't.

Hit the High Points

You're going to be honest about what you've accomplished —but remember that brevity is your friend when writing an engagement announcement. You do not need to list every single thing you've done since graduating from high school— especially if you're something of an over-achiever. Choose the best of your accomplishments and go with them.

 Essential

Your engagement announcement should appear in the newspaper several months before the wedding. Your local paper will give you their guidelines, but a good rule of thumb is three to four months before the wedding.

Listing the six advanced degrees you've earned may be truthful—but it's also a little too much for this particular communiqué. Something will probably be eliminated by an editor who's working with limited space—and it might be the credential you're most proud of. So include *that* one, and let the others slide.

Save your entire academic record for the *other* press release—the one announcing you're being honored as a scholar. Your occupation and most recent degree will suffice for this dispatch.

Second Time Around?

If you or your bride-to-be is getting married for the second time, is it appropriate to put an announcement of your engagement in the paper?

Sure, as long as you're both comfortable with the idea. If she's been divorced and she simply isn't into the whole engagement picture/announcement thing, that's absolutely understandable. Her focus has probably moved from the frills of being engaged to the marriage itself.

If you're the one who's already been around this block, talk to your bride about your reluctance to go the same route again. She may be completely understanding and agree with your opinion.

Be forewarned: As unfair as it may seem to you, she may still beg and plead with you to publish the announcement. Remember, what may seem frivolous to you (the engagement photo, the written announcement) may be part of her big wedding fantasy, and she may not *want* to understand your point of view. She *wants* to see you in the newspaper next to her. You'll need to talk it out and find a compromise.

The Art of Compromise

Whether it's the engagement photo or the announcement, the reception hall or the tuxedo she wants you to wear (the one you have no intention of wearing), the honeymoon plans, or the apartment you desperately want to secure for your life after the wedding (the one she has no intention of moving into, citing "hygiene issues"), life is full of compromises. You're going to learn this as you move further along the wedding planning trail. It doesn't stop once you're married, of course, so *now*—before you walk down the aisle—is a good time to work out the give-and-take in your relationship.

"It's My Way or the Highway"

Anyone who uses this phrase inevitably uses it too much. However, there are appropriate applications for its use. A parent who is corralling an unruly child, for example, might try this demand on for size, and an employer who is running a tight ship might live by this mantra as well. These conditions are well suited for using this particular decree.

It's completely *inappropriate* and unrealistic, however, for an adult to spring this phrase on his or her partner. No matter what the circumstances—whether you feel it's your God-given right to wear shorts to your formal wedding, whether your bride feels she can invite her ex-fiancé to your wedding, when you'd really rather never meet the guy, let alone at your reception—*neither* of you should feel so in control that your future spouse's feelings are of no consequence.

Some issues are obviously more serious than others, but consider the underlying implications of making a unilateral decision about your wedding against the wishes of your fiancée. It simply isn't rational for you to go ahead and do something that you know is going to upset her (if you've come so far in planning a formal wedding, she was probably going on the unspoken assumption that you would wear something *formal*—and not tuxedo-style swim trunks).

Of course, men are not alone in issuing dictates during the wedding season. Brides are often known to turn into alien creatures, ordering their grooms to perform duties that border on slave labor. In the interest of fairness, she shouldn't be doing this to you, either, but the core issue in her demands is likely to be achieving the wedding of her dreams. It doesn't excuse her actions, but if you understand her motivations, you'll have a leg up on working out some of her more outrageous expectations (for example, her idea of "formal wedding wear" is based on Renaissance clothing—complete with tights for you).

 Alert

> Blatantly going against your bride's wishes makes you look as though you're goading her or that you're enjoying her predicament; and it makes you look as though you're living by another mantra: "No one's going to tell me what to do." Maybe the phrase pretty much sums up your entire life—but successful, happy marriages don't run on that fuel.

Sometimes a bride who is spiraling out of control in this way needs a gentle reminder: The wedding is supposed to be about the two of you, and not about her idea of complete perfection *at any cost.*

"Whatever You Say, Dear"

Swinging to the complete opposite end of "compromise," this phrase exhibits a complete lack of interest in the situation at hand. While some of your already married friends may advise you that this is the way out of any potential argument in any relationship with any woman, and especially with your wife . . . ask yourself if this is the way you want *your* marriage to go.

You may argue that your future wife is looking for a fight when she raises the issue of your bachelor party (and how many strippers will be included) for the umpteenth time, and by countering her request (in this case, a request to eliminate the strippers altogether) with a simple "Yes, Dear," you've actually avoided conflict. You're both happier because of it, right?

Wrong. Any wife (or bride-to-be) who hears this phrase from her partner isn't fooled by it—or at least not for very long. When this becomes your response of choice in any discussion initiated by your fiancée, you're going to have conflict. She will realize that not only are you not listening to what she's saying (intentional or not, this is a side effect of using this phrase—there's no *need* to listen when you're going to concede the point anyway), but you probably have no intention of honoring her request.

 Essential

You're not doing your fiancée any favors by pretending to agree with her—you're not doing yourself any favors, either. This is a sure-fire way to break down any intimacy that exists between the two of you.

This phrase really has only one purpose: To avoid communicating with your fiancée.

Since marriage is supposed to be about building a strong alliance between the two of you, think twice before you shoot her down with a "Yes, Dear."

That being said, some brides do wield their veils like sickles, mowing down everyone in their paths simply because the mood strikes them. The engagement ring gives them strange ideas about immediate and complete compliance with their requests. If you recognize your fiancée in this description, you are allowed to use the *occasional* "Yes, Dear" with impunity. Better still, though . . .

Take . . . and Give

Compromise is the core of a successful, happy relationship. One of you shouldn't be doing all the giving while the other does all the taking. Even if you're so in love that this arrangement is working for you right now, things will most likely change down the line. Each spouse needs to know that his or her needs and wishes are respected. No one wants to feel as though they're constantly giving in to someone else's requests.

If you and your bride-to-be constantly spoil each other and won't take a step forward on any issue unless you're both in complete agreement, you're on the right track. Maybe you do give in to her every whim, but she's giving in to your requests, too. Neither of you is getting greedy with demands.

If your relationship has already passed this phase and you find yourselves negotiating every issue for weeks on end, remember this: No one gets their way every time. It's not fair, and it's not right. If there seems to be an inordinate amount of giving on your part (or hers)—or if your discussions go nowhere because neither of you will give in to the other—you both need to take a step back and look at the bigger issues in your relationship:

- ◆ Do you expect too much from her?
- ◆ Does she expect you to agree with every word that comes out of her mouth?
- ◆ Is one of you always expecting the other to comply with every request?

While there are certainly more serious issues that can crop up in a marriage (abuse, affairs, illness), refusing to listen and compromise with each other can set your marriage up for a lifetime of unhappiness. If you're really having trouble discussing big issues consider premarital counseling.

Premarital Counseling

If you're marrying within the confines of a religious community, some churches will strongly recommend premarital classes. Others will require a course to be completed before you can say, "I do." Even if you're not obligated to delve into the most personal issues in your relationship in this manner, it may be a good idea to take a course or talk to a counselor.

What Happens in Premarital Classes?

A group leader will take you through a series of potential problem areas. The larger the group, the more general the presented problems will be—but the idea is to get you and your fiancée talking about certain issues. What are your goals in life? How do you propose to achieve these dreams? Do both of you want the same thing? Are you going to have kids? When? How many? What about money? Who's going to be expected to bring in the dough? Who's going to take charge of the budget? Who's going to pay the bills?

 Fact

As prepared as the two of you think you are for marriage, even the most alert couple can be blind-sided by crises after the wedding. Discussing potential problems—and learning methods to deal with them—can mean the difference between having a successful marriage and having a marriage that doesn't cut the mustard.

The list goes on and on. The big topics in marriage—and/or coupledom—are addressed. If they seem obvious to you, that's good news. Some couples don't address these problems until they come face-to-face with them.

Because many life-altering issues (kids, finances, careers, etc.) are bound to pop up sooner or later, it's a good idea to have a heads-up on what your partner has in mind as far as these topics are concerned. Both of your futures are involved here, after all.

What's the Point?

You're thinking, "So there are a lot of problems in life. Big deal. We'll be fine. We love each other." Love is great, and you need it, but there's more to a happy marriage. Love can fade over time, and if you haven't based your marriage on a solid foundation—i.e., if both of you *don't* want the same things out of life and you don't realize it until some crisis sets in—your happy home will crumble right under your feet.

Think back to the section on giving your fiancée the old "Yes, Dear." You may be tempted to use this line—but is it effective communication? Have you listened to what she's really saying? Have you told her what's on your mind? You've skirted the issue, which may get you off the hook temporarily, but it's not going to be helpful in the long run.

Learning the important skills of effective communication will make your marriage a strong one from the get-go. You may acclimate to married life more easily because you'll know that life *isn't* always sunshine and romance—and you'll have the know-how to deal with those inevitable darker days.

 Fact

The point of premarital counseling and/or classes is to open the door of communication. You'll learn how to talk to each other effectively—and, just as importantly, you'll learn how to listen to what the other person is saying. You'll also learn that conflict is a natural part of any intimate relationship—it's how you resolve the conflict that counts.

Other Issues

So learning to communicate is a big issue here. But learning what makes the other person tick is just as important to a successful union. For example, if your bride pitches a fit every time you have a beer with the guys after work, *why* does she fly off the handle? Has alcoholism been an issue in her family? Did one of her parents have numerous affairs that always started out in a bar?

Everyone has some kind of baggage that they bring into a relationship. Realizing what sets your partner off—and why—is essential to understanding her. If you realize, for example, that taverns mean trouble to her, you're more likely to grasp the magnitude of her feelings, and less likely to think that she's just exhibiting signs of being a control freak.

Something else you'll be asked to consider: What are your expectations of your partner? Are they unrealistically high? (Do you expect your fiancée to pull in $200,000 a year at her nursing job—racking up a *lot* of overtime?) Are they unfairly low? (Do you expect her to cheat on you right after the wedding, because all the women you've ever known have been unfaithful?)

Another expectation issue you may be asked to cover: Do you think marrying her will change her for the better? It isn't fair to ask this of someone. You should be marrying her for who she is now—not for who you think she *could* become in the future.

You may be asked to discuss what this wedding means to each of you. Some couples misunderstand the wedding as the culmination of the relationship (so *this* is what you've been working toward all this time!), instead of the beginning of their lives together. It's an easy enough mistake to make. You spend months (and sometimes years) planning and concentrating on nothing *but* the ceremony and the reception. If no one is there to prod you about what comes next, you may not give it much thought.

Are you both ready for marriage? Are your separate lives (careers, finances, money, health) together? You can't offer much to someone else if your own life is a wreck. Marriage itself won't save you in this situation; it will more likely bring the other person down.

Where to Find Counseling

If you're marrying in a church, ask your priest or minister about premarital education. If the minister himself doesn't offer premarital counseling, many churches offer classes.

If you're not marrying in a church but you're interested in the idea of addressing big topics before taking your vows, you'll probably be looking for a counselor. While this sounds easy enough (they're all listed in the phone book, after all), finding the right counselor is key to your success.

If you don't know anyone who's gone to premarital counseling, ask your family doctor if he can recommend someone. Even if a counselor's name doesn't pop into his mind instantly, he'll know where to locate the name of someone who's reputable in the field. It won't be a complete crapshoot, like picking a name out of the phone book would be.

CHAPTER 4

The Groom's Responsibilities

It may be fair to say that the bride takes on the bulk of planning the wedding in many cases (or she may be stressing over the details, even if she's receiving plenty of help in the planning process). In fact, you might feel as though you've hit the jackpot because it seems as though your bride wants to take on *everything* associated with the wedding, leaving you free to show up and say, "I do." Not so fast. You've got a little work coming your way, too.

The Budget

Taking on some of the planning means that you need to know where you're willing to spend your dough. You and your bride will work this out in one of several ways. You'll take the money you've saved for this wedding, factor in any monetary gifts from your parents, and come up with a rough estimate for how much you can spend on the entire wedding. From there, you'll need to determine whether you're going to spend the bulk of that money on food, on the reception hall, on the bride's dress . . . you get the idea.

Prioritize

As one groom puts it, "Your wedding is all about your priorities." He expounds on this theory by explaining where he and his bride chose to spend their wedding funds—on good food: "If people are going to sit around their tables complaining about the food, what was the point of all the planning and spending? I'd rather serve pizza and have everyone discussing how wacky and creative that was while at least enjoying a meal."

Break It Down

A simple item like the guest list (which is the best item to start with, as a high guest count will cost you big bucks, while a low guest count may be fairly economical) isn't so simple after all. Your caterer or banquet manager will give you a price per guest, or an approximation (a price for 100 to 120 guests, for example). If you plan on feeding and watering your guests (with an open bar), and providing eating utensils and linens for them (as you really should), you'll be shelling out a fairly sizeable chunk of change.

 Fact

There are ways to save. A cash bar, though sometimes unpopular with guests who are expecting free alcohol, is one way to save yourselves a huge amount of money.

So, step one in your Budgeting Extravaganza (it helps to think of it in these terms—add all the fanfare you can muster to the bean counting) is to determine how much you're willing to spend on which parts of your wedding. This takes you right back to setting your priorities. (It's a cycle, see? You can't complete the one part without first addressing the other part.)

And then you must commit to your Wedding Goals. Unfortunately, in the world of wedding planning, you're usually allowed very little "wiggle room." Since so many couples are out there looking for the same services as you and your fiancée, you're at the mercy of the wedding industry. For example, if you book a room for 200 guests and plunk down your deposit (after signing a contract with the caterer, of course), you're going to be held to this plan. You can't decide a month down the road that you would rather put the balance of what you were planning on spending on a reception toward your honeymoon. Bottom line here:

Don't throw any money around until you and your bride are absolutely, positively sure about the expenditure.

 Alert

While some caterers and banquet halls may offer a grace period during which you can back out of the contract, they're usually very short. Once you sign that contract, assume you're going to end up paying the full amount—or, at the very least, a huge cancellation fee.

Organize

Get yourself organized before you talk to any wedding vendors. Even if it's against your nature, even if it's against your bride's nature, it's essential for the two of you to come up with some sort of filing system. You should not take your copy of the receipt the jeweler has handed you and stick it in the glove box of your car. You'll have real problems finding it there if your rings never arrive in the shop and someone wants proof that you've already paid for them.

If you don't have a filing cabinet, choose one spot where you'll both put any wedding paperwork. It can be a desk drawer or a bureau, or a kitchen drawer, as long as it isn't your Junk Drawer. Designate this new spot as your Wedding Planning Headquarters. Better yet, get yourselves a brightly colored folder to slide in the drawer for easy access. Every time you open that drawer, you'll see that folder easily—and that will make placing papers into it that much easier.

Divvying Up the Duties

The bride and her family are traditionally held responsible for the bulk of the wedding and the planning it entails. This includes the reception; most of the flowers; the transportation; the photos and/or video; the music; the dress; and the invitations and announcements.

You're thinking, "Whew! That about covers everything. Guess I'm off the hook."

Hold your horses. There *are* certain responsibilities every groom must address. These include:

♦ The bride's engagement ring and wedding band
♦ Marriage license/officiant's fee
♦ Your wedding wear
♦ Gift for the bride
♦ Honeymoon

Traditionally, the *groom's family* also pays for the bride's flowers, boutonnieres for groomsmen, corsages for mothers/grandmothers, and for the rehearsal dinner. And since most couples these days tackle the wedding planning themselves, you may just find yourself taking on the services that used to lie strictly in Bride Territory, such as finding a good caterer. (More on this in Chapter 5.)

In this day and age, you and your bride might find yourselves scoffing at the "traditional" division of wedding duties, since you may be living together and planning on paying for *everything* out of one communal bank account specifically set aside for the wedding expenses. However you choose to take care of business is *your* business; but if the bride starts feeling a little overwhelmed, you may want to step in and take over where tradition dictates. Many, many brides are happy to plan the whole wedding; some really want help from their man. You know your bride best; do what works for the two of you.

Give Me a Ring-a-Ling

The issue of finding the perfect engagement ring was addressed in Chapter 1. Now it's time for you to take a gander at wedding bands. You are traditionally expected to foot the bill for your bride's rings, so you're going to work with the budget you've established and decide what you can reasonably afford *before* you leave the house.

Plain or with Sprinkles?

If you've already splurged on a big old rock for your bride's engagement ring, you may be planning on buying her a more subdued wedding band. She may be thinking, "More rocks! More rocks!" Since most brides pick out their own wedding bands nowadays, addressing this topic before the two of you walk into the jewelry store is mandatory.

Hers and His

Although the bride traditionally foots the bill for it, you need to choose a band for yourself. Many men make this decision quickly—too quickly—because they honestly don't believe that they are going to be required to wear the thing anyway. After all, your bride understands that you don't wear jewelry.

Well, she won't understand it after the wedding, so you'd best choose a ring that feels good on your finger. Though it may be against everything you've ever advocated for other men, you will need to actually try on some rings before choosing the one that you will wear every day for the rest of your life. Don't make your selection from the jewelry case without even handling it.

 Essential

You'll feel far more at ease explaining your position to her in the privacy of your home instead of in front of the glare of all those diamonds. She'll also be more likely to hear what you're saying if she's not surrounded by cases of jewels—all of them *this close* to being hers!

If you're looking at some very ornate designs, consider whether the ring feels heavy on your finger, if it twists because of the ornamentation, or if it just feels strange to you. Though any ring will take a little getting used to, a ring that is unusually large or heavy may never feel right to you, especially if you're not the jewelry-wearing type.

When making a decision about your ring, consider the following:

- ♦ **Your usual wardrobe.** Are you loving the diamond-and-ruby encrusted look, even though you wear jeans and flannel every day of your life? If it's an out-of-character look for you, pass it up.

♦ **Your line of work.** Large rings may be a hazard for men who work with large machinery. It'll be hard to wear a ring if your finger is missing.

♦ **Any skin conditions.** If you suffer from eczema on your hands, for example, any ring may increase your suffering. Choosing a heavy or ornate ring may drive you to itching distraction for the rest of your life. (Platinum, though expensive, is a good hypoallergenic choice.)

 Fact

Keep in mind that your rings do not need to match. If you prefer the look of plain silver and your bride is into filigree gold, you can each have the ring you want. The important thing is the sentiment behind those bands, not their appearance.

Upping the Ante

Though there's hardly anything more personal than choosing a wedding ring, you can take it a step further to incorporate specific traits of your relationship into this symbol of your union. A custom jeweler or an artist who works in the jewelry trade can help you and your bride choose an unusual set of bands or help you design your own bands. You can incorporate your loves and/or hobbies into a wedding band. You're both into sailing? Choose wedding bands with a wave design. You met while performing onstage? Design a pair of rings with musical notes or a

Shakespearean flair to them. If you share a common ethnic background, you might also consider working a symbol of your heritage into your rings (an Irish claddagh ring, or a Greek key design, for example).

 Alert

You don't need to sit around and wait for the clock to tick away toward your wedding. Even if the big day is six months off, you can get started on this important project. The rings are a vital part of the actual wedding ceremony, after all. You wouldn't want to be without them on the big day simply because you procrastinated.

Is there a ring you've inherited—one that your bride isn't crazy about, because she didn't choose it? Why not include the stones and/or the metal into another, custom-designed ring? In this age of computer design, there's almost no limit to what you can include in your wedding bands. Sketch something out, take it to your artist or custom jeweler, and discuss what she or he can make of it. It's that easy. Deciding on the design is the hardest part.

One caveat: When designing your own rings, it's vital that you start early. Some jewelers working with computer design software may have to send your design out to another manufacturer, and then the ring will be shipped back once completed. Some jewelers may offer "loaner rings" which you'll be allowed to use for your ceremony in the event that your custom rings are not going to arrive in time. Your jeweler may not offer this perk, and in any event, you and your bride may be against the whole idea of "rental rings." Give yourselves a minimum of two months.

Recycled Rings

Another idea for finding a unique wedding band is to start making the rounds at estate auctions. The jewelry you'll find there is typically less expensive than what you'll find in a jewelry store, and especially if your bride is into antiques and/or vintage clothing, you may just find something that no one else can offer—and something you never could have designed.

The Guest List

You've got to come up with a list of people you'd like to see at your wedding. More correctly, you've got to come up with a list of folks who should be invited. You have about fifteen people you're planning on inviting, so you've written down their names and you're all done with this task. Oh, no, you're not.

Call Your Mother

Not just to tell her that you love her, but to ask her which relatives should be invited and which shouldn't. By this time, you and your bride (or your bride and her mother) will have come up with a head count and you'll be able to give your mom a roundabout number to shoot for. Don't beat around the bush here, either. If your half of the guest list allows for one hundred guests, give you mother this very specific limit with which to work. Your mother will also be an invaluable help in gathering up the addresses of family friends and relatives. There are a couple of ways to determine how many guests your family will be allowed to invite. If the bride's family is paying for the reception, they'll probably give you a number. Hopefully, they will be fair about it. If you and your bride are paying, you can take the capacity of the reception hall and divide it three ways: her family's guests; your family's guests; and the guests that you and your bride intend to invite.

The Agony of Family

Unfortunately, in families where there's been a nasty divorce (and remarriages), the guest list is sometimes harder to nail down. Give your mother a third of your family's seats and your father another third and save a third for the guests *you're* inviting. If you need to save half of the seats for your own guests, give your parents each a quarter of the total number of seats. Divide it up however you need to—just be sure that each parent gets an equal share. That way, you can't be accused of playing favorites, and it's really out of your hands. Both parties will be responsible for furnishing you with names and addresses by a certain date; if the deadline isn't met, you can't guarantee those seats for that parent. (You don't want fifty empty seats at your reception just because one parent didn't bother with the guest list—especially if the other parent wanted to fill those seats.)

Who's In, Who's Out

Your mother's boyfriend wants to invite his kids, none of whom you've ever met. Your dad's new wife is inviting her family in the place of your own aunts and uncles. Can you put your foot down? Absolutely. It's *your* wedding. If you see the guest list going awry in the hands of your parents, speak up. You're giving these spaces to them, trusting them to use them wisely. It's not an open party; if the guest list is being filled with people you don't know, nix them right then and there.

Your officiant is invited, as are the parents of your attendants, and the attendants themselves. They should all receive formal invitations in the mail, even though they know darn well that they're on the guest list.

 Alert

You are not obligated to invite kids, and many couples opt not to. If children are going to be included, both families should agree on an age limit, so that the bride's six-year-old niece isn't whooping it up at the reception while your twelve-year-old nephew is left at home.

Coworkers are also iffy, especially if you work in a small environment, and if you fear offending half the office by not inviting them. One solution (though you won't find it in any etiquette books) is to invite those who won't be receiving formal invitations to join you for dancing and drinks later in the evening. It's not *quite* as good as being invited for dinner, but you're trying to include them, and that's the most important thing. Tell them they absolutely should not bring a gift; they should just show up and cut a rug.

Guests of Guests?

Time was, inviting single guests was a breeze. They were either married (or engaged), or they weren't, and that was all the informal distinction anyone needed, at least in terms of excluding a guest's guest. These days, of course, so many couples are living together—but not necessarily officially engaged—that there seems to be no distinction; there's just a gray area where before there were clearly drawn lines.

The predominant etiquette on this topic says that if a guest is married or otherwise seriously involved in a relationship, you must invite both of them. However, this does not mean that you have to let your single friend who dates a different guy every week bring the flavor-of-the-week to your wedding.

Flowers

You're supposed to take care of the bride's bouquet, your groomsmen's boutonnieres, and the corsages for both mothers and the grandmothers. You may, however, want to leave the actual choosing of the flowers to the bride. She probably has a much better idea of what she's looking for in her bouquet, and she may also have very strong ideas about what type of flower she'd like for the groomsmen's boutonnieres.

One way to be helpful here: Suggest looking for a discount or wholesale florist. Then stand back and let her get to work.

You Want Her? Pay Up!

The groom is traditionally responsible for any fees that are connected with the actual marriage. A good rule of thumb here is this: If you absolutely cannot get married without it, it's *your* expense.

License

Every state requires one. Every state charges a fee. Most are under $30, which makes this one of the least expensive elements of your wedding.

 Question

Where does one find information on marriage licenses?
Since every region has its own rules and regulations, contact your county clerk for guidance. The county clerk will be able to explain the requirements you must meet to get married in that state.

In addition to the fee, you'll want to make note of any waiting period that your state may impose. Some states don't require any waiting; some states have waiting periods as long as six days; and in some states, the waiting period only includes *business* days. Do your homework very carefully. You wouldn't want to be turned away at the altar because of a glitch in the paperwork. Best to get cracking early on this project—but not *too* early. The license is only valid for a specified amount of time. Again, this varies, depending on where you live—in some areas, the license remains valid for a number of weeks; in other places, it never expires. You'll need to present the license to your minister or civil officiant (don't forget to bring it to the rehearsal!), who will sign it and send it back to the proper authorities after you've been pronounced husband and wife.

Once part and parcel of applying for the marriage license, a blood test is no longer required in *most* states, so chances are your bride will never need to know that you faint at the sight of needles. (That was close!)

Officiant's Fee

You are responsible for handing over the cash to whoever is pronouncing you husband and wife. This is a flat fee—no tips are required. You may want to give the envelope with the dough inside it to your best man, who will then hand it over to your officiant.

Rehearsal

This is where you'll get your bearings and realize that yes, you *are* getting married. You'll have a run-through of the entire ceremony with all of your attendants and family members in their places, and you'll follow it up with a meal of some sort. You can go very casual (pizza, wings, and beer), or you can make it a formal affair in a nice restaurant. This is a good time to hand over the marriage license and to pay the minister.

Who comes to the rehearsal and the rehearsal dinner? Anyone who's playing a crucial role in your wedding. This includes both sets of parents, siblings, grandparents, attendants, your officiant and his or her spouse. If your attendants are bringing dates to the wedding, you may want to include them in the rehearsal; some couples also choose to invite any out-of-town guests. If you have a ringbearer or flower girl, they will need to attend the rehearsal in the company of their parents.

Wedding Night

You'll also need to make arrangements for your wedding night. If you're flying out of town the next morning, you might want to stay as close to the airport as possible. If you've got a few days to put your feet up and relax, you might be looking for deluxe accommodations.

Hotels

If you're simply looking for overnight lodgings in town, chances are you won't have time to even step foot on the balcony of your hotel room, let alone take advantage of any honeymoon packages. You'll arrive late in the evening, completely exhausted from the reception; you'll wake up in the morning and you'll be on your way. Look for something reasonably priced, and skip the extras.

If, on the other hand, you have the entire weekend at your disposal, ask your hotel if they offer a honeymoon package. This may include an upgraded room; champagne;

room-service breakfasts and dinners; massages; souvenir bathrobes, and those tiny little chocolates on your pillows before bedtime. (All this and cable TV? Who needs to leave town?! You've found the perfect honeymoon spot!)

 Fact

A small inn can be incredibly romantic—but be aware that everyone knows your business in a place like this. The walls are thin, for one thing, and there's much less anonymity than you'll find in a larger hotel. If you're passing through on your way to other accommodations, an inn might be fine for a night—but for a longer stay, or for your actual wedding night, think *private*.

Home Sweet Home

It may be more practical and economical for you to spend your wedding night in your own home, especially if the two of you have been living together before the wedding. You have everything you need right there, after all; you won't have to lug your suitcases to the reception; there's no hassle of checking in; you'll both sleep well in your own bed; and you don't have to worry about tipping anyone.

If you're going all-out on your honeymoon expenses and you just can't justify spending your wedding night in a top-dollar suite somewhere across town, no one says you have to. You've already established the perfect little newly-wed nest; no sense letting it go to waste.

Honeymoon

No, it isn't enough just to book the hotel for your wedding night. Grooms are traditionally held responsible for planning the honeymoon, as well. Chapter 8 covers this in much more detail. For now, be aware that you're the Go-To Guy on this project. Put your thinking cap on. Some of the most popular honeymoon destinations include Europe; Hawaii; the Caribbean; and cruise ships.

You might be thinking, "We don't want a popular spot—we want seclusion!" Popular doesn't necessarily mean overrun. What you can almost bet on with a popular honeymoon spot, however, is that it's geared toward people like you—couples who are looking for a little rest, relaxation, romance—and fun. So if "popular" doesn't appeal to you, try to think of these destinations as "practical"—everything you want in one place.

The Bride's Gift

You thought *you* were her gift! Well, of course you are—but to commemorate this major event, the beginning of your lives together, you might want to give her something else. It should preferably be something that will stand the test of time, and something that will have some special significance to her.

Drawing a blank on what to give your bride? (Gee, you thought she'd really like those socks you gave her for her birthday, and she acted like she was expecting something *more*.) Some ideas:

- **Jewelry.** Give her a pair of earrings that she can wear on your wedding day.
- **Art.** Is she looking for just the right painting to hang in your home?
- **Furniture.** Antiques are a nice touch here—something that has already stood the test of time.
- **Other ideas that suit her.** Is she into gardening? Find a sculpture that will complement her plantings. Picture frames are beautiful and practical (especially since you'll have scores of wedding and honeymoon photos to display). She's really wanted a mink coat for a long time now, hasn't she?

She's already been inundated with household items, so a toaster is definitely not something you should wrap up for her. Avoid grabbing something at the last minute—put some thought into this. And don't give her cash. (For tips on *when* to spring this gift on her, read Chapter 10.)

If you really want to spoil *all* of the most important women in your life, go ahead and pick up a gift for your mom—and your mother-in-law, too. You can buy them earrings or watches; they'll also appreciate a picture frame or a hobby-related item. Don't get them the same gift you buy for your bride, and do try to keep the gifts for the mothers in the same price range. Present the gifts from you and your new bride at the rehearsal dinner. This will go a long way toward creating one big, happy family.

Being the Rock

Above all, your main responsibility is to provide all the love and support you can for your bride during this planning period. You may think that you're feeling the stress of this wedding, and you could use some support yourself—and that's what *she's* there for. Be aware, though, that most brides take wedding mishaps and stresses more to heart than men do. This all goes back to little girls dreaming about their perfect weddings, while the little boys are off doing something else. When the dream starts unraveling, even a little, there can be big trouble.

Listen

When your fiancée is telling you for the umpteenth time that she can't decide on the color for the bridesmaid dresses, don't turn your back on her in favor of watching the game on TV. This may be old news to you, but it's a big deal to her. (If you want to make it a *bigger* deal, try ignoring her.) Remember that you're entering into a lifelong partnership with this woman. This is just the tip of the iceberg.

Talk

Offer her some sympathy. Remind her that this wedding is ultimately about the two of you spending forever together.

Tell her you love her, you love the wedding plans, and you think she's beautiful even when she's crying.

If you've got some wedding headaches of your own, offer them up and commiserate with your honey for a while. Maybe the two of you will decide that you should scale this wedding down to a more manageable size; maybe you'll work out some alternate plans; or maybe you'll realize that this is just part and parcel of planning the big wedding. Whatever the case, you'll realize that you're in this together—which can be a great comfort in times of upheaval and stress.

CHAPTER 5

The Big Picture

You're getting into the actual planning, which includes making real (and sometimes difficult) choices, but this is also the fun, exciting part of planning the big day, so take the leap with your bride and don't even try to hide that smile. This chapter will give you an overview of the various wedding industries that are out there waiting for your business, as well as how to interview a prospective vendor. Think of this as a little treasure hunt.

The Church

Be aware that choosing a church isn't always as easy as it sounds. Some churches are booked solid months in advance, others have special requirements that couples must meet before they can walk down the aisle. And what if you and the bride are from different religious backgrounds?

Waiting and Waiting . . . and Waiting

Many churches have long waiting lists, some as long as several months, during which time you may also be required to attend premarital classes or counseling. Give yourselves plenty of time if your heart is set on a particular church; being flexible doesn't hurt, either. (If the waiting period determines that you'll miss out on a Spring wedding this year, maybe a Fall wedding would be just as lovely.)

If you or your bride has a minister who is almost like family and you can't imagine getting married without him or her presiding over the vows, get on the horn right away. Give him or her plenty of time to work out a date with the two of you. Although this clergy member *is* family as far as you're concerned, he or she does have an entire congregation to take care of; a good minister can't put off a previous engagement just to show up at your wedding on a week's notice.

Religious Conflicts

You're from a family of atheists; your bride's clan are devoted Christians. Can you two bring a couple of hundred philosophically and theologically opposed wedding guests together for a peaceful evening? No, it's not the premise for the next big reality television series, it's your wedding day! When you and the bride are of very different religious backgrounds, how can you put together a wedding that will please everyone?

First, you have to decide whom you're trying to please. If having peace in the family is extremely important to you (and to many couples it is), then you might try a hybrid ceremony, where a civil officiant (a judge or a justice of the peace) and a religious cleric (or clergy from each of your churches) stand side-by-side and pronounce the two of you husband and wife.

 Alert

Combining religions or officiants in one ceremony isn't always an option, depending on which religions you're trying to merge. Talk to your officiant as early as possible about what you'd like to do.

In some instances, one partner may decide that the religious issue just isn't that big a deal and will agree to be married by the other's choice of minister (civil or religious). What's most important here, though, is that the final decision is made by the two of you—not by your mother, not by your fiancée's mother, not by one of your grandmothers. The choice to please all of the important people in your life is a noble one; the choice to remain true to your beliefs is noble, too.

If you choose to be married in your fiancée's church and you don't belong to her particular religion, you may be required to follow a set of guidelines before the minister will consent to marry the two of you. This may be as extreme as converting to her religion, so you'll have a lot to think about. Again, make sure the decision is *yours*. You shouldn't be going so far out of your way to please her parents that you and your own family are left scratching your heads, wondering, "How did all of this happen?"

Civility

A civil ceremony is usually much shorter than a religious one. Think of it as the streamlined approach to saying your vows. That's not to say that you can't include your own touches: Writing your own vows, for example, or including some special music.

 Essential

If you plan on adding personal details to your wedding, you should inform your officiant well before the ceremony. He may be running on a tight schedule, and you don't want him slipping out the back door before you've said, "I do."

A civil ceremony can usually be performed at the site you've chosen for your reception, though in some localities, there may be restrictions. (Check with your county clerk and your reception site.) The benefit of this, of course, is that your guests won't have to worry about a delay between the ceremony and the reception, and you won't have any downtime between the two events, either.

Before You Go Any Further . . .

You've already discussed the budget and organized yourselves—now, try to do some research—*before* you make appointments to talk with the caterer or the limo company. Check out these businesses, first by logging onto the Better Business Bureau site and also by asking around.

You shouldn't assume that because a company has not had a formal complaint lodged against it that it is a reputable business (your complaint may be the first), nor should you assume that a company with one or two formal complaints is disreputable (not every customer is sane and rational).

Word of mouth—if you can find it, and especially if it's from a source you happen to trust—is a great indicator of a business's true colors.

Stand Your Ground

Avoid giving in to high-pressure sales pitches. In the end, this is a business deal. You are paying these people to perform a service for you; they are not doing you any favors by taking your money, even if they present the situation in this light. You may feel squeezed by certain vendors; take your time in deciding what's right for you and your wallet.

What will you do, for example, if you're meeting with the hottest band in town and the leader tells you that there's another couple interested in the same date you're thinking about? And this other couple is going to call him later in the day to book the band? What you're not going to do is beg *him* to book *you* right then and there.

 Fact

Being pressured into something may cause you to second-guess your decision. If you and your bride have already decided that booking this band is your top priority, you obviously won't hesitate to sign on the dotted line, but if pressure is the selling point, think twice.

Sign Here . . . In Blood, Please

Before you sign any contract with a vendor, read it in its entirety—yes, including the fine print. (You'll find the most interesting reading in those teeny little words.) Don't accept your caterer's word as Gospel Truth when he nonchalantly tells you that it's a "standard contract." Make sure that it doesn't include any clauses that favor only his business in the event of an unforeseen catastrophe, for example.

Look for a clearly stated contingency plan (for example, what happens if your DJ falls ill the day before your wedding?). Do not sign or hand over any money until you are satisfied with the terms of the contract. And if you can't come to terms with a merchant, keep looking. You'll save yourself a lot of grief if something should go awry.

Remember: Contracts always favor the merchant more than the customer. That's the reason for their existence. If the contract in front of you favors the merchant in a wildly unfair manner (if the contract states that the vendor shall receive full payment even if they go out of business before your wedding date, for instance), think twice before signing it. Obviously, if this is the reception hall you've both wanted for years, you're going to jump through hoops to book it. Just be careful. Don't be so blinded by your wedding fantasies that you lose your shirts in the process.

 Essential

No matter how friendly the interviewee seems, no matter how cooperative, insist on seeing the refund and cancellation policy in writing—*before* you sign anything. The written word is the final word in this situation.

Receiving Your Guests . . . Somewhere

Choosing a church—as difficult as that experience can be—is a cakewalk compared with finding a reception hall that suits your every wedding need (the need for good, reasonably priced food and drink, the need for clean surroundings, the need for plenty of ladies' bathroom stalls). This experience often ends up being the most time-consuming, most expensive, most frustrating part of planning a wedding. This section offers up a little advice in how to choose the right spot for you.

Narrowing Down the Choices

You won't choose your reception site from the Business Listings in the phone book. That's a perfectly acceptable way to choose a dentist or a mechanic, but this is your wedding. You need to ask around—get some real opinions of the reception places in your area.

You need solid anecdotal evidence here, and it's easy enough to find. Even if none of your friends have taken the plunge into marriage yet some of their family members have. Some of their other friends have. You have relatives who can tell you about their wedding experiences. All you need to do is ask. Most people will be more than eager to offer their take on the whole thing.

ⓔ Alert

Combining religions or officiants in one ceremony isn't always an option, depending on which religions you're trying to merge. Talk to your officiant as early as possible about what you'd like to do.

If you're looking for a nontraditional reception and someone can tell you about a certain place (a picnic grove or an old converted theater, for example), you'll be able to get a feel for the entire experience—which may help you decide if you'd rather go the traditional route, or if you want to have a more creative wedding day.

The Array of Choices

Finding the right reception spot is essential to the good vibes of your wedding. The wrong place can ruin the whole day. The problem is, every place you and your fiancée have discussed looks great. How do you get down to brass tacks and find out which place is the right place? A few well-phrased questions can narrow down the list fairly quickly:

- How long has the place been in business? How many events are typically held there each year? What size?
- How many guests can the facility serve?
- Does the facility have an on-site caterer? Are outside caterers permitted?
- Does the facility have a liquor license?
- Where's the dance floor? How big is it?
- Where will the musicians set up?

Get an itemized list of what the price quote includes. Are linens, tables, and chairs included or will they cost you extra? Is there a cake-cutting or champagne toasting fee? Is there an extra charge for setup and cleanup? Is gratuity included in the quote?

The Caterer Interview

If you decide to work with a caterer, you'll want to be prepared with a list of questions. A few to throw at him/her (the last five also apply to the on-site caterer at a reception site):

- Is this person a full-time caterer?
- How many servers will be at the wedding? How will they dress?
- How long has the person been a caterer? How many events has the person done? How large an event can he or she comfortably handle?

- Does the person have any type of formal training?
- Does the caterer have a liquor license? A health permit?
- Will a bartender cost extra?
- Is it possible to book a "taste consultation"?
- Is gratuity included in the price quote?

These questions will get the conversation rolling, and from there you can move on to other topics, such as your wedding cake (does this caterer provide one, or will you need to find a separate baker? Does this caterer charge a cutting fee for an outside cake?) and your payment schedule (will you have to pay the total at one time, or in installments?).

Entertainment

You're going to want to get your guests up and grooving at some point in the evening. A reception without music is like a summer night without crickets—there's just something missing without background noise. Will you choose a band, a DJ, a string quartet, or your own mix of music?

DJs

One perk of hiring a DJ is that he will probably have the latest, hippest, now-est music, and will therefore be a big hit with the younger crowd. For these same reasons, the older crowd may be turned off by him or her. If you're going to be inviting a lot of elderly relatives, ask your DJ if he has a collection of standards—Big Bands, Sinatra, and the like.

When interviewing a DJ, ask for a sample play list. If he's into hip-hop, and you're Country through-and-through, keep looking for someone whose tastes (and music library) are more similar to yours. Ask him for some references, and ask about other weddings that he's been booked for. Check this guy out thoroughly. Music makes or breaks a party, so you want to know that this guy is going to get the job done right.

 Fact

Can't decide whether you'd prefer a DJ or a live band? This might help: DJs are usually much cheaper than bands. Some DJs also offer karaoke, which is just the thing to get your guests up out of their chairs.

You'll want to ask about the DJ's experience; how many hours he will spin the platters at the reception; how he will dress for your big day; whether he has appropriate music for your cocktail hour; and if his price quote includes gratuity.

Live Music

Maybe you're thinking you'd like a live band instead of a DJ. If you've already heard them play at another function, (and this is where you got the great idea to hire them for your own wedding), your work is done. Call them, book them, high five them. If you're going on the recommendation of a friend or relative, you're going to have to hunt these musicians down and hear them play.

If you decide they're competent musicians and they're welcome to entertain your guests, you'll meet with the business head of the band and discuss the music for your reception. Be aware that although you may have your heart set on a particular song for your first dance with the bride, the band may not include this particular song in their repertoire. You may have to be flexible.

If you're planning a luncheon or afternoon reception, you might want to consider a string quartet or a jazz ensemble. Your guests won't be expecting to hit the dance floor before dark, and you'll be providing them with some easy listening.

 **Essential**

If it's at all possible, try to listen to any band you're thinking of hiring in a venue that's similar to your reception site—live music can sound wildly different indoors, outdoors, in large, cavernous halls, and in cozy little spaces.

No matter which music you're leaning toward, you should check out the DJ or the musicians in person before you sign a contract with them. Whether they're appearing in a club or at a function, you should be able to see them at work before you give them the green light for your reception. Try to catch them on at least two occasions, to make sure that their amazing performance last weekend wasn't just a freak accident.

The Photographer

For all but the smallest weddings, a professional photographer is usually needed to capture the essence of the day—the bride gathering with her attendants; the groom waiting nervously in the church; the guests whooping it up at the reception. You want to know that you're going to get your money's worth. What will you ask your prospective photographer?

For starters, ask about his or her experience (how many weddings has this person done?) and/or education (did he or she study photography in college, for example?). This is not the occasion to give an aspiring photographer a chance. You want someone who knows what they're doing. You should also ideally try to find someone who takes pictures for a living instead of a hobby. (Yes, the guy who does this as a hobby will be cheaper—but the quality of your pictures may turn out to be much less than you expected.)

Ask how many pictures he will take; when he'll take them (some photographers like to scoot out of the reception as early as possible and will insist on staging certain events to meet their own timeline) and who will determine which photos will end up in your wedding album. Most photographers will give you the proofs to choose from, but some photographers choose to skip the whole proof process and will choose your pictures by themselves—a plus if you have a hard time making decisions; a minus if you end up with a lot of pictures of people you don't know. Ask to see samples of the photographer's *recent* work.

Transportation

The bride's family is traditionally responsible for covering the cost of transportation on the big day. If you're the one who's *actually* paying for it, you'll have some research to do before you choose a vehicle. While limos have had their day in the sun, there are many other options available for shuttling your entire crew around from the church to the picture sights to the reception.

Limos

Once available in regular and stretch, you can now super-size your limo ride. Today's super-stretch limos can seat twelve or fourteen of your closest pals. Most up-to-date limos will include media entertainment (in the form of a state-of-the-art stereo, DVD player, and TV), telephones, and neon lights. You probably won't need all of this for a short ride from the church to your reception, but it's nice to know it's there if you want it.

Many limousine companies offer wedding packages, which will typically include champagne, a red carpet, and a set number of hours. You will be required to pay hourly for any amount of time over and above the package price. Three hours may sound like plenty of time to you right now, but on your wedding day, you may need that limo for five or six hours (depending on any delays between the ceremony and the reception).

If you need an early morning lift to the airport to get started on your actual honeymoon, many limo companies offer this service as well.

In the event that you don't want to break up the wedding party into two separate limousines, some livery companies can now offer you modified SUVs that will seat more than twenty of your closest pals.

 Fact

Some limo companies also offer "reception service," which means that you can keep the driver on the clock in the event that some of your guests need a ride home from the party. You and your bride will be the last guests shuttled off, on your way to the Honeymoon Suite.

Another option is to hire a party bus, which resembles an airport shuttle, and has plenty of room for the entire wedding party to move about the cabin. If you choose to hire an old-fashioned trolley, you'll find comparable seating and lots of fresh air.

Going in Style

Even if you think a limo or a trolley is the best choice for your wedding party, you're not bound by any sort of wedding by-laws to travel with the gang. After all, this is your wedding day and the only person you want to be with is your new wife. Consider hiring a classic car (like a Rolls Royce or a Bentley) for you and the Mrs. to ride in while the rest of the gang fiddles around with the moonroof in the limo. Or perhaps you'd like to travel from the church to your reception by horse-and-carriage.

Checking Things Out

Before you hire any sort of transportation service for your wedding day, do your homework—thoroughly. Again, you can start with word-of-mouth recommendations, but that's not nearly enough. You'll want to go and see the fleet of limos (or the horse that's supposed to pull your carriage) with your own two eyes. Any reputable limo company will not hesitate to allow you to inspect their vehicles.

 Alert

One thing men often overlook—and one thing that will matter to the women in your bridal party: Cleanliness and style. Are you surrounded by crushed velvet? Is there any possibility that this car was once used in the illegal solicitation trade? Pass it up.

Ask about their maintenance procedures—how often are the limos serviced? Are they insured? Look carefully at the license plates. Are they "Livery" tags? How do the cars look from the outside? Do they appear to be well cared for, or are there scratches and dents all over the doors?

Now get in. Stretch out. Take a look around. Don't be afraid to ask for a test ride. At the very least, the manager or owner of the company should be willing to start the engine so that you can see that everything is in working order. You don't want to find out on your wedding day that the stereo doesn't actually work, or that the TV isn't real. Take your time.

If the limo is squeaky clean, it's modern, everything works, and you can just see yourself sitting there in your tuxedo, flashing your new wedding ring . . . this may be the car for you.

When checking out a party bus or a trolley, similar rules apply. While you should expect a certain amount of cleanliness (and absence of odor), you can't expect a huge vehicle like this to be detailed the way a car can. Again, feel free to ask for a ride around the parking lot. Is there smoke coming from the engine? Does the vehicle lurch violently when shifting gears? These are utilitarian transports, for the most part—you want a big vehicle your whole wedding party can sit in. Style falls by the wayside. (A nice plus, to be sure, but hard to find in large-sized shuttles.) What you're shooting for is reliability. Ask for references.

Signing the Contract

So you've checked out this particular limo in a fleet of twenty. How do you know that *this one* is the one that will arrive to pick you up on your wedding day? Get it in writing.

Some companies may lease limos from another company, and therefore may not be able to guarantee you much of anything, let alone which car will show up at your home. Try to find a company that has its own fleet of vehicles. These companies know where their cars are going (and when), and more importantly, where they've been. The owner of a limo company is going to keep his cars in good repair—it's *his* bread and butter.

Some companies have vanity plates on their limos—this is how their limos are easily identified. For example: You've just checked out the most unbelievable limo—you'll accept no substitutes. Whoever writes up your contract (the owner or the manager) should write the plate number on your contract: "ABC 1" or "ABC 12," or whatever the number happens to be. (And where are you going to put that contract once you've signed it? Into your Wedding Headquarters File.)

Other points to look for in the contract:

♦ **Time.** Number of hours you're paying for up front, and the hourly charge after that.

♦ **The driver's attire.** Most companies will outfit their drivers in tuxes for a wedding. Make sure this company follows suit.

♦ **Contingency.** What if "ABC 12" has an accident the day before your wedding? If you're paying absolute top dollar for this particular car, will a partial refund be made?

♦ **Gratuity.** Is the tip added into the contract (a nice plus if you don't want to be bothered with it later; a minus if you get lousy service on the wedding day), or will you be required to fork it over to the driver yourself?

The Driver

Whether you're hiring a limo, a trolley, a horse and carriage, a classic car, or you've asked your cousin to drive you around in his van, you need to recognize the driver as a human being and *not* as your slave for the night. Yes, he (or she) has been hired by you to cart you and your pals around. No, this person should not expect to take a whole lot of abuse from you.

Though this poor driver is used to seeing his fair share of drunken revelers, you may not address him as "Jeeves." You may not moon him through the glass partition. You may not incessantly page him on the intercom and tell him to "put the hammer down, 'cause Smokey's in the woods."

Above all, remember to tip your driver well (fifteen to twenty percent of your total bill), especially if you have ignored the previous admonitions.

Buyer's Remorse?

You've set your priorities, you've signed some contracts, and now you're thinking you were all wrong, that you've planned a wedding that's completely wrong for you, you'll never be able to afford all of this, and you don't know what the two of you were thinking in the first place.

Don't give in to self-doubt. Take a minute to look at the big picture. In addition to taking a huge step in your personal life, you're also forking over a lot of hard-earned money in the process. It's normal to feel as though you've made an error in judgment along the way, at least as far as budgeting goes.

Stay calm and remember: If you've done your research and you've taken your time making decisions, you've eliminated the potential for a lot of error. Any mistakes that crop up will most likely be flukes and you can look at them as learning experiences.

CHAPTER 6

Men in Penguin Suits

You'll choose your own side of the wedding party—but how? You can't possibly eliminate any of your close friends, family, or coworkers . . . or can you? Next you'll look for the right tuxedo for you and your band of men. Choosing the right wedding wear depends on several factors: The type of wedding you're planning; the time of day you're planning it for; and, of course, cost. And what if you're not planning a traditional wedding? This chapter also offers suggestions for the path less traveled.

Choosing Your Attendants

Your bride had to whittle her list of potential bridesmaids down to a manageable number. Now it's your turn. Though you'd like to include your family, your childhood friends from the neighborhood, your high school buddies, your fraternity brothers, and your new best friends from work . . . some of these men won't make the final cut.

Thicker Than Water?

Start with your family. If you have brothers, you're probably going to want to include them. The exception, of course, is if you and your brother(s) despise each other. Another exception may be if there's such a large age gap between you and your brother that he's more of an acquaintance than a sibling. When there's a big family or age issue between you and your brother, he might be more puzzled than honored if you ask him to stand up for your wedding.

 Alert

If you choose not to include your brother(s) in your wedding party, you may have to contend with other members of your family who feel you're slighting your kin. Listen to any unsolicited advice patiently—then make the decision on your own.

If you're on the fence about including a distant brother in your wedding lineup, consider the potential long-term advantages. This may be just the thing to get the two of you talking. And though a large age gap means a generation gap when you're young, that gap tends to narrow as you both age.

The Bride's Bros

Don't forget about your future brothers-in-law. As long as you and the bride's brothers aren't life-long enemies, your list of attendants should include at least one of her male siblings. While you have some discretion where your own brother is concerned, excluding the bride's brothers from your side of the wedding party is going to be an issue with someone in her family—and probably not with the brother himself. More likely, the bride's sisters or her mother (or her grandmother, or her aunts) will be distressed by your decision. By excluding the bride's brothers from the wedding party, you'll be starting off your new marriage with one strike against you as far as the bride's relations are concerned. (At least if you offend a member of your own family, you know how to deal with them afterward.)

If the bride has five brothers, however, you should not feel obligated to ask all of them. Ask for her guidance in choosing who should be fitted for a tux.

Friends

Here's where feelings can be hurt. By choosing some friends and not choosing others, you're bound to offend someone. Still, you can't have everyone parading down the aisle, so choose you must.

Your bride will have chosen her attendants by now, so you'll have a number to work with, if you are concerned about having even numbers on both sides (which, of course, is not essential). Excluding family members, you'll only have a few coveted berths open for friends to fill in the Groomsmen category.

 Fact

Choose your men carefully, keeping in mind that each attendant will be required to shell out some substantial bucks to cover the cost of his tux, any travel expenses, the bachelor party, and a wedding gift. Family and close friends won't consider this an imposition; acquaintances might.

New friends should be the last on your list, especially if they're very new (you've known them a year or less). There's just no telling if this friendship will stand the test of time, and you don't want a wedding album filled with pictures of "that guy."

Your boss should also be fairly far down on the list, no matter how close you feel to him. Anything can happen in the business world, and on the off chance you're downsized in the future, you don't want a wedding album filled with pictures of the guy who did the shrinking.

Friends who have been in your life for a good, long time—men you trust, men who respect you—should be tapped to stand beside you at the altar.

Sorry, Dude

What kind of friends should be excluded? Unreliable friends (someone who might pack up and leave town the week before your wedding); friends who don't like your bride (your attendants are supposed to bear witness to this union and support it, after all); friends who will be put out by the whole affair (the friend who will complain bitterly about the cost of renting a tux); friends who are potential troublemakers.

Take, for example, the story of Snake, the Grooms-man. Snake stood up for Michael at his wedding several years ago. Although he was an obvious partier, Michael did not learn until his reception that Snake was into illegal narcotics (when a man arrived to "do business" with Snake).

 Fact

If you have reservations about a pal who just might end up being a Snake at your wedding, it's best to leave him out of the loop. Sure, he might be mad—but the friendship just might end *anyway* if you do include him and he ruins your reception.

By the end of the evening, Snake was so out of control he had to be carried out and thrown into a cab by the groom himself, who shudders when he looks at the wedding pictures now. "All I think about when I see these pictures," Michael says, "is how badly this guy offended my guests. I never spoke to him afterward, and there he is in our wedding album."

If you still find yourself with too many pals and not enough spaces at the altar for each of them, consider asking a friend to do a reading instead of being a groomsman. Ask another friend to help bring up the gifts in the church. You can also include some male friends as ushers—they'll dress the part, but they won't stand at the altar.

Who's the Man?

After choosing the groomsmen, you're going to have to pick *one* of them to be your best man. Most men don't lose a lot of sleep over this issue, but if you have three best friends to choose from, it could be a tough call.

You've got to have a best man—there's no way around it. One way to narrow down your options is to realize that the best man is actually *responsible* for quite a few things:

- He's supposed to organize your bachelor party.
- He should help you corral the other groomsmen into the tux shop.
- He should help you supervise the other attendants on the wedding day.
- He needs to get you to the church on time.
- He's responsible for hanging on to the rings, the marriage license, and the officiant's fee.
- He gives the first toast at your reception.

The best man is tasked with standing by you throughout the wedding season. Make sure you choose someone who is up to the challenge. If you're choosing from several friends and only one of them is adult enough to handle these tasks . . . your choice is easy.

Some men choose their dad to be the best man. You might want to think twice about this, especially if the rest of your wedding party is following a standard route. Is your dad really going to feel comfortable spending the day with your rowdy pals? Is he really going to host the kind of bachelor party you want? Would he rather sit with his wife at the reception than at the head table?

If your wedding is small, your dad might feel very comfortable playing the role of best man. Otherwise, let him opt out. The same advice applies if you're thinking about asking your child to fill the role.

Ringbearers and Junior Groomsmen

If you have a (much) younger brother or a favorite nephew or a friend's child who is *like* a nephew to you, you may want to consider including the youngster in the wedding party as a ringbearer (a job for the very young—think eight and under) or a junior groomsman (something every eight-year-old ringbearer aspires to be). The young man (or men) will dress the part and stand at the altar during the ceremony (if his age allows this for kind of patience).

Stressed out over this choice? Too many kids in your life? Well, there's good news and bad news, depending on how many little guys are in line for the role. You can include more than one junior attendant in your side of the wedding party, but *three* should be your absolute limit. Should the ringbearer or junior attendant come to the reception? Ask his parents. If he's a very little tyke, he probably won't last long anyway, but if he's nearing middle school, he might cut a rug with your bride all night long. In any event, his parents may or may not want him at the reception, so let them make the call.

 Essential

Young children should not be subjected to the drinking and adult behavior that sometimes goes on in the limousines between the ceremony and the pictures and the reception, so you should make arrangements for them to travel with their parents after the ceremony.

Attendants' Gifts

You'll also have to reward all of your groomsmen for a job well done. As a token of your appreciation for their service in your wedding, you will be required to buy gifts for your attendants (and ushers). Since this is a special event, you should consider purchasing gifts that they will actually keep and use. Don't give them dress socks to wear to your wedding. (You *could* purchase them some nice ties, however.) Some ideas:

- Money clips
- Watches
- Pewter or silver key chains
- Flasks
- Cufflinks
- Shaving kits (nice ones—not the kind you'd pick up at the drugstore)
- Golf balls (or good fishing lures, or a gift certificate to a "manly" store)
- Gift certificates for an upscale men's salon
- For the kids: Gift certificates to their favorite restaurant or a special toy should suffice

What to Wear

Your tuxedo salesman wants to know what kind of wedding you're planning, how many guests, what time of day. Is this guy nosy or what? No, he actually isn't. He needs to know these things so that he can set you up with an appropriate outfit. He does not want you showing up to a formal wedding wearing that snakeskin tuxedo you've been eyeing in his shop. That's the kind of word-of-mouth advertising he doesn't need, and your bride will have a few words for you, too, if you show up dressed inappropriately.

As good as you're going to look (and you know you are), the fact is that your tux and your groomsmen's tuxes will pale in comparison to the outfit your bride has chosen for herself. Tuxes don't draw a lot of attention, generally speaking—unless they're completely *wrong*. Think low-key (though not invisible) when choosing your outfit. This is not the time to make a bold fashion statement, especially if you've never made a fashion whimper in your life.

 Alert

If you have any doubts about the ensemble you're putting together, give in to those doubts. Better to err on the side of caution than to end up regretting this particular wardrobe choice forever.

What Kind of Wedding?

Is it formal, semiformal, daytime, evening? What difference does it make, you ask yourself? Snakeskin tuxedos go with any décor, any time of the day. Keep reading. Please.

Your main choices for categorizing your wedding:

♦ **Daytime semiformal.** Your good dark suit should suffice. Your groomsmen should dress as similarly to you (and to each other) as possible. In the summer months, you can consider lighter colors or fabrics (linen, for example).

♦ **Evening semiformal.** You can opt to wear your suit to this wedding, or you can choose a black tuxedo. Add a cummerbund and vest, a bow tie, and a white wing-tipped shirt.

♦ **Daytime formal.** Here's where you start dressing the part of a movie star! Gray or black jackets (cutaway, strollers, or tails are all acceptable); striped trousers; vest; striped tie or ascot.

♦ **Evening formal.** "Black tie." Black tux; white shirt; black bow tie (or a four-in-hand); vest or cummerbund.

♦ **Daytime very formal.** Black or gray cutaway coat; gray striped trousers; vest; ascot; cufflinks; gray gloves. Add spats and a top hat at your own peril.

♦ **Evening very formal.** "White tie." It doesn't get more formal than this. Black tailcoat; black trousers; white wing-collared shirt; black vest; and yes, a white bow tie.

Vocabulary

That's fine and well, you're saying, but what the heck is a wing-collared shirt? (It's a formal tuxedo shirt with a triangle-shaped collar . . . that kind of looks like an origami bird. Kind of.)

Other common shirt types include:

♦ **Mandarin collar** (i.e., no collar at all—no tie needed)

♦ **Spread collar** (has a wide space between the points of the collar in front)

♦ **Crosswyck** (crosses in front)

♦ **White pique** (refers to the fabric and is very formal)

Then you've got the jackets:

♦ **Tails.** They've got tails. A fairly formal look.

♦ **Tuxedo.** Your basic tux jacket. Single- or double-breasted with a slew of lapel choices.

♦ **Mandarin.** Stand-up collar, minus the lapel.

- **Cutaway or morning coat.** Short in front, long in back.
- **Stroller coat.** Actually a semiformal suit jacket cut like a tuxedo coat, for daytime wear.

And then . . . you have *more choices*:

- **Double-breasted.** No, it's not a medical condition. It's a jacket with two rows of buttons. Single-breasted coats have a single row.
- **Lapels.** You've got your notch, your peak, your shawl, your Mandarin. A quick overview of these: Notched lapels are notched and are commonly seen on single-breasted jackets; peak lapels come to a peak and are commonly seen on double-breasted coats; shawl lapels are rounded (like a shawl); and Mandarin jackets have no lapels at all.
- **Cummerbund.** The pleats should face *up*. If you're against this practice, choose a vest.
- **Accessories.** Bow ties; gloves; cufflinks; shoes; top hats; canes. These can make or break your appearance. Use your best judgment. If your tuxedo salesman is trying desperately to talk you out of (or into) something in this area, listen to him or her. Remember: There *is* such a thing as Wedding Day Over the Top Wear.

You Want More?!

You want a better idea of what you should wear? Look to your bride. Your tux should complement her dress. If she's planning on wearing a hand-beaded frock with a ten-foot train and a floor-length veil, you'd better not show up in your linen suit. The gasps from onlookers will be audible.

You shouldn't expect your bride to hand over a picture of her gown, but she should be able to give you some idea of where she's headed with that dress.

Tux Shop Hunting

Should you just pop into the first tux shop you come across in the mall? Probably not. Though tux shops might all appear to be exactly the same, they aren't. They may differ in price, quality, and—most importantly—service. If you run into a problem with the tuxedos the night before the wedding, you want to feel comfortable in the knowledge that your tux shop will take care of it. It's not worth saving $20 on the rentals if it means all of your men will be wearing different suits at the altar.

References

Your best bet for finding a good tux shop is a good reference. Ask friends or family members about their experiences with a certain shop. Were they given the correct tuxes—and all the accessories—at the time they were promised? Did the shop offer the entire group any discounts? Did the store seem up-to-date, or were there some questionable-looking threads hanging around?

See for Yourself

Don't take someone else's word for it entirely, though. Go into the shop and browse around. Check out the quality of the tuxes on display; note the helpfulness of the staff, too. (If they aren't any help to you now, they sure won't be any help if you have any last-minute problems.) Take a tux for a test drive in the dressing room. (Try out some of your dance moves, if space permits.)

 Essential

> While price might be an important consideration, this is one area where you might get exactly what you (don't) pay for, in the way of cheap duds or bad service.

If you can't find any obvious flaws with this shop, and you've come here on the recommendations of a friend or two, you may have found your place.

Get Measured

You should really start looking for your own tux three or four months before the wedding. This will not only give you plenty of time to choose the ensemble, it will give your groomsmen plenty of time to get measured for their tuxes.

You'll be measured in the shop by someone who knows what they're doing. He or she will measure your inseam, your waist, your jacket size. Ideally, your groomsmen will be measured in the same shop, but life isn't always cooperative. Still, your groomsmen should also be measured by professional tailors—even if they live out of the area.

The worst thing that can happen is that your best man will send his measurements—which he took himself—and the tuxedo shop will order him a tux that will never, ever fit him. He won't know this until he arrives in town the day before your wedding and tries on this tux. Maybe the shop can find him another tux; maybe they can alter this one; and then again, maybe they can't. Maybe he'll just end up wearing something completely different from the rest of the wedding party. Yep, he'll stand out, all right—for all the wrong reasons.

You should really rent the shoes from the tux shop. Their dress shoes are very different from the dress shoes you and your buddies wear when you're out on the town or in a business meeting. The wrong shoes will ruin your entire look.

 Fact

Giving your tux shop measurements that are way off is as useless as telling them to order whatever size they want for a particular groomsman. Make sure your pals understand this.

Cost

While some etiquette and wedding books will steer you toward paying for the entire wedding party's tuxedo bill, this one won't. Realistically, most attendants will expect to pick up the tab for their tuxes. That's not to say that they will be happy about paying for *all* the extras—the top hat, the spats, the cane (no one could talk you out of those, huh?).

If you're going the whole nine yards, you might want to consider picking up part of the bill. Otherwise you may find yourself at the altar wondering why no one else is wearing spats.

Tuxless Weddings

So what if you're not getting married in a semiformal setting? What if you're getting married in a field, or on a beach, or at the top of a mountain? You know you're not wearing a monkey suit while you hike for hours and hours . . . so what will you wear?

The Outdoorsy Wedding

If you're getting married in a field of wildflowers, in the garden, or in the grove, your wedding is probably geared toward casual dress. Casual doesn't mean you can sport a pair of cutoff shorts and flip-flops, *especially* if your bride is planning on wearing something lacy. (If *she's* wearing cutoffs, you're off the hook.) You're going to have to dress nicely or she may come to a screeching halt at the far end of the aisle.

If you have a good suit, it'll work here. If the setting is casual enough, you can even wear a sports coat and pants. Your groomsmen should be dressed similarly—to you and to each other. Pressed white shirts, conservative ties, dress shoes, and matching socks. Groom yourself well (no pun intended). You don't need a tux to look like a million bucks, but you should put your best foot forward today.

Beach Weddings

If you're getting married in a sandy locale and you just can't see getting saltwater and grit all over your good suit, talk to your bride. If she's planning on wearing the big white dress and the veil, you *have* to look like the groom she's going to meet—and not like the cabana boy who's hoping to sweep her off her feet. These will not be wedding pictures that either of you will cherish.

If she's willing to scale back her attire (she doesn't want to fuss with yards of satin and tulle in eighty-degree weather, for example), then you're on to something. She may opt for a much more casual look—a simple, lacy dress, or a gauzy skirt. Then—and only then—you can consider a less formal look for yourself, like a pair of linen pants and a lightweight shirt.

CHAPTER 7

The Mother(s) of All Headaches

Ah, your future mother-in-law. Can't live with her . . . and nothing more needs to be said, as far as you're concerned. Or is it *your* mother who's a little out of control over this wedding? Are both mothers duking it out with *each other*? Throw a stepmother or two into the mix and the event you are planning looks less like a wedding and more like a military maneuver. Whether you come out in one piece on the other side is up to you.

Your Mother-in-Law

Dealing with your future mother-in-law during the wedding season can feel like you're negotiating a minefield. You mention the band you'd like to hire for the reception and *BOOM!* While dining with your in-laws, you're describing the tux you're thinking about wearing to the ceremony and *BOOM!* You sit down to work on the guest list and *BOOM!* There are ways to successfully negotiate the triggering devices; you only have to be an active participant and willing to go the distance.

She's Footing the Bill

If you and your bride have gone the ultra-traditional route and her parents are paying for most of the wedding, you're in a spot. Yes, it is your wedding, but no, you will never convince your mother-in-law of this fact when she's the one signing the checks.

In fact, if she's pretty much taken over the entire planning process of this wedding, she's probably also the one who's done all of the legwork—whether or not you wanted her to. She's put her time *and* her energy *and* her money into this production, so she's probably not going to be very receptive to your opinions at this point.

To be fair to your bride's mother, try to see things from her point of view. This may be extremely difficult, especially if she's been snippy with you lately, but give it your best shot. She sees you and your bride as *kids,* for starters, and she's treating you to the equivalent of a big old day at the amusement park. Imagine the reaction you'd get if you complained about the rides, the food, the weather, and the entertainment options at the park. She'd be sorry she brought you, and what's more, she'd probably tell you to shut your trap.

 Fact

You need to come to some sort of arrangement concerning the wedding planning with your mother-in-law early on. You can't leave the wedding planning up for grabs and suddenly announce—after she's done all the work, and when the wedding is next week—that you had every intention of getting involved.

Much larger scale: Your wedding. If you have been sitting on your haunches up until this point, *allowing* your mother-in-law to run the show, saying very little until she's actually interviewed nine caterers and hunted down the perfect band, you're going to get the same reaction, which is, simply put (in your mother-in-law's voice), "Who the heck do you think you are, you little whippersnapper?"

Chances are, if your future mother-in-law has put a lot of time and money into planning your wedding, your bride has allowed this to happen, too—which means you're not going to get much in the way of support from her if and when you decide to voice your opinion on the reception hall your mother-in-law has *her* eye on.

Nipping Trouble in the Bud

Fortunately for you, there is a way out of this quagmire. Unfortunately, it's going to cost you.

Telling your mother-in-law straight out, as soon as that ring is on your fiancée's finger (or soon after), that you plan on taking an active role in the planning may lead her to point out that she's the one with the big bucks—and that she expects her daughter to walk down the aisle in a certain *style*. Here's where you keep your cool and remind this woman that it's your wedding, too, and that you fully intend to shell out some big bucks of your own (at least they're big as far as *you're* concerned).

If she intends to pay for the whole thing, and planning isn't really your thing, this may be a match made in heaven. However, if your two strong personalities are going to be butting up against each other from the minute you propose until the morning you leave on your honeymoon, it's best to be honest from the get-go—before your mother-in-law spends a single dime.

And if she plays the victim and refuses to shell out *anything* because you've cut her out of the loop? Roll with it. Consider it destiny. You may not be able to afford a lavish affair, but think about the peace of mind you're going to have knowing that you and your bride planned the wedding of your dreams—instead of playing roles in the wedding your mother-in-law wishes *she* could have had.

Let It Slide

Mothers of the bride are quite susceptible to falling prey to temporary insanity when a wedding season rolls around. Suddenly, your bride's mom may seem like a complete stranger to you. This woman who seemed to like you (up until now) has strongly-worded rebuttals to your opinions and is planning a wedding that bears little resemblance to anything you had in mind. Will this go on forever? Should you speak up? Are you her puppet on a string? (The answers: Probably not; Sometimes; and Not Really.)

Things That Matter

There are some areas of the wedding planning that strictly belong to you, as the groom, and unless you voluntarily forfeit them, your future mother-in-law should not usurp these domains. These include:

♦ Choosing the groomsmen
♦ Choosing the tuxedos
♦ Picking the bride's wedding band
♦ Your choice of guests
♦ The vows
♦ The rehearsal dinner locale
♦ Honeymoon preparations

For example, your mother-in-law shouldn't object to your brother as the best man (because she'd really like to see her own son in that role), nor should she book the country club dining room for the rehearsal dinner without first asking your family if they'd like her to. She shouldn't be inviting 120 guests to the reception while allowing your family to extend invitations to fifteen of your closest relatives and friends.

This is all within the realm of etiquette and fair play, and chances are, most mothers-in-law wouldn't dare risk the hard feelings that are associated with a hijacking of this sort. If your bride's mother feels that she should be planning every part of the ceremony——even those that are specifically *yours*——you have every right to speak up and object.

 Essential

Keeping quiet about big issues *now* (when the lines are clearly drawn by tradition and etiquette) could set you up for a lifetime of dealing with an overbearing mother-in-law (the lines are a little harder to see when life settles into an everyday routine—and your mother-in-law is still trying to run the show).

Not Worth the Fight

Because this is your wedding and everyone's emotions are out of whack, issues that normally wouldn't bother you might just pop up and cause you severe distress. In some families, *any* wedding issue can be turned into a raging war. Remember: Many wedding arguments are not worth the oxygen they deplete from the atmosphere. Things that fall into this category include:

♦ Beef vs. chicken at your reception
♦ The color of the limos
♦ The color of either mother's dress
♦ The flavor of the wedding cake (unless you have an allergy, of course)
♦ The song for the bride's dance with her father (which her mother has chosen)

The reasons you should let these things slide? First of all, if she's bothering to make an issue of these items, she's probably paying for them.

Secondly—and more importantly—these are things that won't bother you on your wedding day. You're going to be so busy posing for pictures and greeting guests that you may not have time to taste the food on your plate, let alone acknowledge it as poultry or beef. If your mother-in-law wants to wear a polka dotted dress to your wedding, who cares? Black or white limos will be equally pleasing to you as you get in one of them with your new bride, and you'll have a new appreciation for carrot cake when it has a bride and groom posing on the top of it.

Mother-Bride Tension

You're dealing with your future mother-in-law just fine, you say. The two of you have come to an agreement—you're planning your part of the wedding, she's planning her part, things are moving along smoothly . . . except the *bride* is ready to do away with her mother and give it all up—the wedding, your future together—for a berth in the Big House. How can you help?

The Benefit of Your Wisdom

Since you're obviously holding things together pretty well, be the calming force in her life. Don't raise your excitement level to match hers when she complains about her mother. Listen to her, but don't hop on the Judgment

Train. Brides can get a little crazed during the engagement season, which means that her arguments might seem a little empty to you. (Her mother refused to pay $3,000 for the wedding cake? Sounds reasonable to you—but wow, is your fiancée angry.)

 Alert

This is not the time to tell your bride that she's veering into bratty territory; however, presenting a logical argument might do wonders for her perspective. Pointing out to her that $3,000 will go a long way toward paying for the wedding pictures, for example, just might bring her back down to earth.

Running Interference

If the situation devolves into a mother vs. daughter grudge fest, you're obligated to take your bride's side—no matter how badly she's treating her mother, no matter how strongly you disagree with her behavior. Here's why.

First, siding with her mother is only going to put you in the doghouse with your future bride. She won't be speaking to either one of you, which leads you to the second reason why you need to stick close to your bride, especially if and when she turns on her mother during the planning phases of the wedding: Assuming you're not at odds with your future mother-in-law, you are the link between these women.

Siding with the bride doesn't mean that you need to treat her mother as badly as she does. It simply means that you'll lend your girl your ear when she needs to vent. If you really don't feel that her mother's actions border on criminal, keep it to yourself—but treat her mother as you always have. If you can keep the relationship between your future mother-in-law and yourself on an even keel— without crossing over into what your bride might consider Enemy Territory (in other words, no private meetings with her mom), you might be a powerful example for both of these women.

 Essential

If the bride and her mom are battling over the wedding, her mother won't be expecting a great deal of support from you—so imagine how pleased she'll be when she realizes that you're actually a rational human being. This is going to go a long way toward creating a happy future with your in-laws.

Your Sweet Mother

Heretofore, your mother has always seemed like the ideal woman to you. She has never been what you would call *pushy*, she always listened to your opinion, and as for your bride-to-be . . . gee, the two of them got along swell before you popped the question. So what's up with your mother badmouthing the bride? Is there a reason your mom has a problem with the entire wedding, start to finish? Can there be a rational explanation for why she continues to shoot down everything you're trying to tell her?

Can her behavior be explained? Yes. Will you like the explanations? Probably not.

You're Her Baby Boy . . .

Whether you're the firstborn or the last of the litter, you're always going to be your Mama's baby. No matter how old you get, she's always going to see you as a child. You know this much already.

 Alert

Don't give in to the temptation to actually be a baby boy. You have thought this through and you know that you and your lady are ready for the ultimate challenge of lifetime commitment. That's all you need to know about yourself in this situation—that's everything.

What you may not realize is that your mom has serious doubts about whether or not you're ready for Real Life. College is one thing; working for a *Fortune* 500 company is another; taking on the responsibility of a wife and a home (and kids, perhaps, down the road) is a whole other ball of wax. Your mom has been there; she's raised the family; she knows how hard it is—and she knows that no one ever realizes what the job entails until you're smack dab in the middle of it. If you're on the youngish side, she might be worried that you'll long for the single life once you're paying a mortgage and committed to coming home after work every night.

Continue to act like the adult that you are, and don't fall into your role as the Baby, even if you think it will make your mother happy. This will only give credence to her doubts about your readiness for marriage.

And remember this: Even if your mother really loved your fiancée while the two of you were just dating, that engagement ring can do a number on Mom's sanity. Previously, your mother didn't feel as though your loyalties were divided—obviously (in her mind, at least), family comes first. That diamond (or ruby, or sapphire) has expanded your family and your obligations. Your wife will now come first in your life (though if you're not careful to make this very clear to your mom, this may be an issue for debate for years to come); and what's more, you're going to be expected to divide your time between your own family and your bride's family.

 Fact

Speak up on behalf of spending time with your own family. If your bride doesn't think it's important to you, she may not make the effort; after all, it's always going to be easier for her to spend time in her own parents' home.

This shouldn't be as hard as it sounds; most couples find a way to work family issues out, by splitting up visits over the holidays, for example. (If you live out of town, you'll visit her family for Thanksgiving and your family for Christmas, and switch holidays the following year so that no one is offended—or you'll just stay in your own home, or you'll work out something that suits the two of you and your situation.) To be on the safe side, you and your bride should work out the issue of holidays and family visits before it becomes an issue with either set of parents.

Your mom is afraid of losing you to the other family in your life. There is something you can do about this, however. Some men let the bride take over and end up spending an extraordinary amount of time with her family, giving credence to the old adage, "A son is a son till he takes a wife; a daughter is a daughter all her life."

Feeling Unneeded

If you have a sister who's already been married, your mom went through the whole planning process with her—and she was looking forward to your wedding, too, until she realized that this isn't her event to plan. Now she's just downright surly whenever the topic of the wedding is brought up. She feels as though she's been knocked out of bounds on this one—and she's right. Traditionally, the bride and her family take on the bulk of the wedding and the planning.

This doesn't necessarily mean that your mom has to sit on her hands throughout the entire planning process. The bride and her family may really appreciate any help your mom can give them, especially if your mom has been around the Wedding Planning Block and they're still novices.

Attention, Please!

Alas, what can be done about a groom's mother who intentionally tries to—or succeeds in—sabotaging the wedding so that the spotlight will be drawn to her? It depends on the infraction.

One groom remembers that when the limo arrived to take him and his parents to the church, his mother—who is a big attention-seeker—suddenly couldn't find her shoes. Since she was wearing a very formal tea-length gown, the shoes were of the utmost importance, and she refused to leave the house without them, which was no big deal, the groom thought, because they had plenty of time before the wedding. It wasn't long, however, before the groom realized that he was going to be late for his own wedding—and he saw the simple solution:

"We looked for those shoes for half an hour," he says, "and they were nowhere to be found. Finally, I looked at the clock, and it hit me that I had to be at the church—I couldn't stay another minute. I said, 'I gotta go. Come to the church when you find them.' *Then* she remembered that she had left her shoes in the trunk of her car so that they *wouldn't* get lost in the house. She wanted to show up late to the church to make my fiancée worry, and also to make a late entrance, so that everyone would be so relieved that *she* made it in time. Not that the wedding could start without *me*."

The Wildly Inappropriate Mom

This groom lucked out in that there was no other option, as far as he was concerned, other than leaving his attention-seeking mother at home, shoeless. His mom's actions, while certainly annoying and selfish, were fairly limited in scope. What can you do about a mother who is bound and determined to be nasty to the bride's family, or worse, resolute in her convictions to put on some sort of freaky show on the dance floor during your reception?

 Alert

> If you want to get your mom involved in planning the wedding, proceed cautiously. Your bride and her mother probably have very definite ideas about this wedding—which may not resemble *your* mother's views. Your mom (or you) should be prepared to pay for the areas of the wedding that are handed over to your family.

Tough love. This is *not* your mother's day. If she can't behave, she has to leave. No ifs, ands, or buts about it. She can be angry with you from here to eternity; that's her prerogative. But as your mother, she's your responsibility. Don't make your bride have a word with her; don't force the bride's father to drag your mom out the door. If you sense she's got something up her sleeve, be prepared. Have the number of a cab company, and use it at the first sign of trouble.

Mom vs. Mom

In this corner, your mom is weighing in at a respectable undisclosed weight, wearing a blue silk floor-length mother of the groom dress; in the opposite corner, your future mother-in-law is weighing in at a very similar respectable

weight, wearing . . . the same exact dress as your mom. Oh,
heavens. Can these ladies come to a truce before the wedding? Let's hope so.

It happens sometimes that the mother of the groom and
the mother of the bride won't see eye-to-eye on anything.
It could be because they're of different socio-economic
groups; it might be because they're from different generations; it could be because way back in the 1980s, one of
them did something to offend the other. (And who knew
that you and your bride would insist on getting married one
day and force them to speak to each other?)

 Essential

If your fiancée's mom is bold enough to comment on
your parentage, speak up on your own behalf—the first
time it happens. There's no room for negotiating here.
This is offensive behavior, and you are not obligated to
tolerate it in the name of not making waves.

No Trash Talking

First things first: You have a vested interest in getting
along with your own mother and your future mother-in-law.
Make it very clear to your own mother that you do not want
to hear her bad-mouthing the bride's mom. You will, after
all, be spending holidays with this other woman.

Opposites Don't Attract, Silly

Sometimes opposites like to stay . . . opposite one
another. And that's fine. No one should ever feel as though

they need to change to please someone else. In the case of two mothers who can't seem to get along, however, they may need a little shove toward one another.

Here's an idea: Set up a lunch date with you and your bride and your mothers—pick a restaurant that's convenient for both mothers (or equally inconvenient for both). The benefit of eating somewhere other than your home is that when lunch is over and the check is on the table, you can easily signal an end to the afternoon.

🅔 Alert

Only attempt a meeting of the minds if you're dealing with two women who are willing to give peace a chance. Otherwise, you could leave the table with severe indigestion, realizing that the situation has only deteriorated.

Lunch can be as quick—or as lengthy—as you want, so it's a better choice than dinner (which can drag on and on) for this particular meeting. There will be less time for awkward silences—and yet plenty of time if everyone is getting along terrifically.

Even if these women believe that they have absolutely nothing to talk about, you and your bride can prove them wrong. Steer the conversation toward neutral territory. All mothers love to talk about their kids. Ask your mother-in-law about your bride when she was a child (even if you've already heard the stories from your fiancée); make sure your bride is prepared to draw your mother into the chitchat. Initiate a conversation about the food, the surroundings, the weather—anything that is nonthreatening.

Both mothers may be surprised to find that they can, in fact, talk to one another, and they might even discover that they have a few things in common. (Stranger things have happened.)

Stepmothers

Many, many couples find that when planning a wedding, they're forced to deal with the issue of mixed families—and they have no idea what to do. After all, when the first etiquette books were written, divorce and remarriage were not acknowledged, let alone given space in print. These days, of course, ignoring the issue of divorce and stepparents is impossible—and cruel. You may love your stepmother as much as your own mom—but how can you include her in your big day without stepping on any toes?

Evaluate the Family—Honestly

If there are big problems in your immediate family stemming from your parents' divorce and remarriages, this is not the time to ignore those issues or to say to yourself, "Well, they're just going to have to get along on my wedding day." If there's tension between your mom and dad (or your mom, dad, stepmother, and stepfather), the last thing you want to do is to put anyone in a situation where that tension is going to be on display or exacerbated to the point of an ugly confrontation.

Don't expect miracles just because you're getting married. Don't seat your parents together in church—or at the reception—in the hopes that your wedding will be the balm for their catastrophic relationship. You're thinking, "They'll all be so moved by the ceremony, everyone will walk out of the wedding the best of friends." No, they won't.

Remember that weddings tend to get the best of people who are normally rational. Your parents may be forced to do battle with conflicting emotions on your wedding day—joy (as they watch you standing at the altar, waiting for the love of your life); fear (that your marriage won't fare any better than theirs did); and pure animosity (when they catch each other's eye). Give them plenty of space to hold themselves together.

You Sit *Here* and You Sit *There*

Don't seat dueling parents and their new significant others in the same pew in church—unless you want to hear from one of them that they really would have preferred the aisle seat. Give them both aisle seats, one behind the other. That's about the best you'll be able to do without holding separate ceremonies for each parent.

Put each parent and their new spouse at a separate table—preferably nowhere near each other—during the reception. Seat them with other members of their own family (your grandparents, aunts, uncles, etc., from your mom's side will be seated with her)—and if there are still seats left over (if your mom has a very small family, for example), then fill out the seating arrangement with a few of her close friends.

Keep in mind that as much as you'd like them to put their differences aside for this one day, they may be too far gone to comply. Your mom and dad may not be able to enjoy themselves if they're forced to be in the vicinity of one another. Make things easy for them—and, more importantly, for yourself.

Appeal to Their Sensibilities

Before the ceremony and the reception—well before the big day, talk to each of your parents. Be completely honest about your concerns, but don't get into placing blame on either of them. The issue you want to resolve before the wedding is whether both of them can agree to either call a truce or simply ignore each other for a given number of hours on a certain Saturday in June. Impress upon each of them how important it is to you to have a peaceful wedding day. You don't want to hear their complaints; you don't want to hear them bickering in the vestibule of the church.

Stepsiblings

Of course, along with stepparents, sometimes there are stepbrothers or stepsisters thrown into the mix—and the mix isn't always a good one. Do you have to invite a stepsibling you've never liked (or one you barely know, for that matter) to your wedding?

The answer depends on how you want your familial future to proceed. True, you may not be especially fond of a stepsibling or two, but they do fall under your family umbrella.

Whether you're debating over *not* inviting your mom's stepson or your dad's stepdaughter, one of your parents has to deal with this child (or adult) on a fairly regular basis—and with this child's *parents*, also. You and your bride will be the hot topic of conversation between all of these folks for a good long time if you choose to exclude a stepsibling. You're not just proving a point to the stepsibling in question—you're putting your own parent in a tough spot, too.

 Fact

Your best bet is to let each parent and stepparent know exactly where they will be seated during the ceremony and the reception. This will eliminate any wedding-day objections or protests from the peanut gallery and all you'll have to worry about is showing up at the church and looking good.

Of course, your family relations may be so poor and your reasons for slighting a stepsibling so valid that you really don't care who will be angry over the whole situation. That's something you have to evaluate on your own. Just be aware that you're putting yourself in the position to have guilt and blame heaped upon you for years to come.

If you can possibly find it anywhere in your being to include the stepsibling you despise, you'll take the attention off of yourself. The ball will be in his or her court, and you will be absolved of any wrongdoing. If he or she doesn't respond or refuses to attend the wedding, you can just shrug and say, "Hey, I *tried.*"

Mingling Before the Big Day

This chapter already covered how to get two very different moms talking. But what if your families have never met? If you're living on the West Coast, and your family is on the East Coast, and your bride's family is overseas, chances are these people have never laid eyes on one another. And if your bride's family *is* from another country, are they going to think *your* family is completely nuts?

Start Small

A good way to get the families together is to invite them to your home—wherever that is. You shouldn't ask your bride's family to meet the two of you at your parents' house, for example, as it may make them feel extremely uncomfortable, and it also may imply that your family has the "home field advantage." The exception to this, of course, is if a trip to your parents' is going to be much more convenient for international travelers—and your parents are open to hosting everyone.

Culture Clash

So you're getting the folks together and you're losing sleep over the possibility that one set of parents will perceive the other set as strange?

Don't borrow trouble, as the saying goes. Most adults—especially in a situation like this—will really try to make things work. Unless your parents are unusually disagreeable folks, or unless her parents spout prejudicial rhetoric on a daily basis (situations where you'd be right to be concerned, by the way), count on each party being on his or her best behavior.

 Essential

You don't want to overplan a Get-Together Weekend, but you don't want to underplan it, either. Find some activities in the area; take them on a tour of your city; go out for dinner. Keep everyone busy enough so that any awkward silences can be interpreted as pure fatigue.

If things do go horribly awry, there's not much you can do about it, anyway. These people are adults, after all, and they're capable of taking care of themselves, even in the face of extreme rudeness. You can take them so far on this journey, by planning, by initiating certain safe topics of conversation . . . but you can't orchestrate every moment of this meeting. And in the end, if they find they aren't going to be the best of friends, that's all right—so long as no one is trying to stop your wedding.

CHAPTER 8

Honeymoon Preparations

Lucky you, you get to take care of the fun part of the wedding—the vacation. If you've never planned a night away from home, let alone a trip across the state line, you might feel overwhelmed. Then again, you and your fiancée may have been all over the world already—so where should you go for your honeymoon? With a little creativity and a little help, you can plan an extraordinary trip for the two of you. You just need to dive in and get to work.

Picking the Place

It might be very difficult to narrow down the exact right spot for the two of you. What if, for instance, you love the mountains, and she loves the ocean? Or what if you've had your heart set on traveling across Europe while she'd much rather check things out Stateside? Is there any middle ground? Can your honeymoon be saved?!

No-Go's

Before you dismiss your fiancée's hatred of hiking and plan a trip to the Rockies, think the entire thing through. Is there a *reason* she hates being out in the woods, climbing toward a summit? Does she have allergies, for instance, or asthma—things that would make a honeymoon in the mountains treacherous for her?

If she's determined to check out the southwestern United States when you're really shooting for Asia, is it because she has family in the area? Are the two of you always on the lookout for an interesting place to move, and she's been talking about Albuquerque a lot lately?

She may have something in mind when she's suggesting potential honeymoon spots. Before you go ahead and surprise her with a honeymoon she might hate, *ask her* what her thoughts are. If you have an interest in scuba diving and she's really looking forward to a golf vacation, you can find a spot that will please both of you.

Now, if she's looking to spend a week on the slopes and you want to hit the beach, the planning might be a little trickier—but here's where the art of compromise—

and picking the right location (like California)—comes into play.

 Fact

Even if you've already hit every corner of the world, don't feel as though there's nothing special left for the two of you to discover on your honeymoon. You're in a perfect position to re-visit the spot(s) that you found most romantic.

Popular Destinations

Honeymooners are usually looking for several things in a trip: Sun, romance, relaxation (reading, shopping, spa visits, etc.), adventure (sports, gambling, camping, etc.), culture (museums, shows, etc.). Depending on your personalities, you and your bride-to-be may be looking for one or all of these traits in a destination. Some of the most popular honeymoon sites include:

♦ Mexico
♦ Caribbean islands
♦ Tahiti
♦ Aruba
♦ Hawaii
♦ Europe
♦ Florida

Of course, anywhere the two of you go will be a honeymoon destination, so don't feel pressured into choosing a place simply because hordes of honeymooners have gone before you. (Don't shy away from a place for that reason, either. Resorts that cater to honeymooners usually know a thing or two about making each couple feel special.) Think about your own wants and needs and go from there—and don't be afraid to use a travel agent.

 Essential

Communicate. Sounds like a simple enough plan, but some couples have a problem clearly stating their expectations and/or wants, opting for the old, "Oh, whatever you want, Hon," response—and speaking up only when it's too late. Communication will make your planning infinitely easier (by narrowing the list of choices from the get-go).

Consider whether you're looking to travel a good long distance, or whether you'd like to stick near home. Know what your budget is. Have an idea of what you'd like to do on your honeymoon (Relax? Ski? Swim? Visit museums? Shop? Hit some nightclubs?), as your interests will dictate the location. Are you interested in an all-inclusive tour or resort?

This information should help you eliminate a big chunk of the world; your travel agent can help you choose from the locations that are left.

Cutting Corners . . . *Carefully*

If you've looked at your budget and decided that you can only afford to hit the road if you scale things way back, do so at your own peril, recognizing that traveling standby in the days following your wedding may cost you what precious little sanity you have left at that point.

Jennifer tells the tale of her honeymoon ordeal, which started out in a grand fashion. Her father had given her and her new husband passes to fly anywhere—the catch was that the tickets were only good for standby seating. The newlyweds planned a trip to Hawaii in June, figuring that because they were traveling in the off-season, they would have no problem reaching their destination.

 Fact

Computer savvy, are you? If you're completely comfortable with booking a trip online, go for it. Some of the best bargains are out there for you to hunt down from the comfort of your ergonomic chair.

Jennifer recalls: "We forgot to figure in all the connections we had to take to get to Hawaii, which ended up being quite full. Our journey ended up consisting of these flights: Buffalo to Chicago. Chicago to San Francisco. San Francisco to Los Angeles. Los Angeles to Honolulu. Honolulu to Maui. And we ended up buying tickets for the last leg of the flight (Los Angeles–Honolulu, Hawaii) because twenty-four hours had passed and we just couldn't take it anymore.

"Not to mention the fact that on the first day of travel, we were running on literally two-and-a-half hours' sleep and had nasty little hangovers, which made my mental state a bit unstable. I burst into hysterical tears after the third Chicago–California flight took off without us on it." Her suggestion?

"If you're going to cut corners, be mentally prepared for the unexpected. Keep in mind that it may be a little too much to handle after all the wedding stress, and that it might be worth the extra money to go with trusted airlines, accommodations, or resort packages. Even if you *don't* cut corners, inconvenient things happen—consider *that* carefully if you're going to tempt fate even more."

Fortunately for Jennifer and her husband, both of them bounced back from the travel trauma once they were able to settle into their ocean-front digs. If you or your bride is not the type who recovers well from bad travel experiences, plan yourself a foolproof trip instead of looking for creative ways to pay less. In the end, it'll be more than worth it.

Covering the Bases

Before you commit to any location, do some further research into the area and the trip. Your travel agent should be able to tell you whether your trip will fall during the rainy season (or hurricane season, for that matter); he or she should also be able to check and see if there will be any construction going on in the area during your stay. You don't want to be awakened each day at seven in the morning by the sounds of jackhammers and bulldozers building a new road through the jungle that surrounds your posh hotel.

Ask about any charges you'll incur for changing your dates of travel or your flight times. These charges can add up to a hefty amount, so if there's any possibility of your changing your plans, tell your travel agent up front.

 Alert

Due to the new security measures at airports, airlines now recommend that brides traveling the day after a wedding (or anytime before they have changed their names on their photo IDs) have tickets booked in their maiden names, as a valid photo ID is required in order to board a flight.

All-Inclusives

An all-inclusive tour or resort vacation will include the price of your room, food, drinks, and (often) sightseeing trips. You might think that this pretty much takes care of the whole expense of the honeymoon, but there are other expenses that could put your budget over the limit:

- ♦ **Airfare.** Is your airfare included? If you're going on a tour, how much will you pay to fly from your city to the tour's point of origin?
- ♦ **Travel.** Is transportation from the airport to the hotel included? Is there a hotel shuttle to take you into town to eat and shop? If you're forced to rely on taxis, this expense can really add up.
- ♦ **Gratuities.** In many all-inclusive resorts, the gratuities have already been added in to your bill. Don't double-tip.

Cruises

The food! The drinks! The casinos! The shows! No doubt about it, when you choose to cruise, you're taking a trip that includes just about everything. To make the most of your floating honeymoon, follow these tips.

Find the Right Ship

Understandably, your first concern is the destination—but ask your travel agent to put you on the ship that will suit your needs. Do you want to be onboard a twenty-four-hour party ship, or are you looking for something a little quieter? Many cruises offer similar services (spas, exercise classes, shows, gambling, etc.), but the extent to which each of these services is offered on your particular cruise may or may not be to your liking.

 Essential

Keep your carry-on bag after you get off your flight. It can take hours for your bags to find their way to your room, and you'll want your swimsuit and your sunscreen handy when you board the ship.

Book Early and Don't Be Stingy

Reserving your room early—at least four to six months prior to your honeymoon—is the cheaper way to go. And don't listen to anyone who tells you that your cabin doesn't really matter because you'll be so busy, you won't have time to be in there, anyway. You're going on your honeymoon. Chances are you will be spending a good amount of time in the cabin. If you have the means, book the room with the veranda so that you can sit and watch the sun set . . . and rise.

Most cruise lines will provide you with their own guidelines for tipping, but the cardinal rule remains the same whether you're on land or at sea: Tipping is always at your discretion.

Europe

If you're off to an English-speaking country in Europe, you may feel as though it's no big deal. They're just like us but with accents, right? (Ooh, there's that American Attitude.) Tips for traveling in Europe:

Know the Culture

Don't walk around France expecting everyone to speak English and refusing to eat in any restaurant that doesn't serve cheeseburgers. You're looking to create an international incident with this mindset. (If you want American food and English-speaking folks, wouldn't it be a lot easier to stay in the United States?)

On the other hand, if you're looking to get intimately acquainted with European culture, look for the smaller, out-of-the-way places. Don't book a room at the biggest chain hotel; instead, look for a small inn (aware, of course, that you may trade your privacy for the cultural experience). Dine at restaurants that don't cater to tourists. You'll definitely get a truer feel for the region if you aren't searching for a café with golden arches.

Other Things to Know

Europe is a hotspot for American tourists. Avoid falling into the stereotype of the ignorant American tourist by following these tips:

- ♦ The off-season in Europe is from October to April. You'll find better deals then, and you won't find yourself in a crowd of Americans—in the middle of Rome.
- ♦ Have cash on hand if you plan on hitting the smaller inns or restaurants. Many of them don't accept credit cards.
- ♦ Check on any vaccinations you'll need, and if you haven't seen your dentist in a while, do so before you leave. (You'd hate to have a tooth give out in Warsaw, wouldn't you?)
- ♦ Learning a few basic questions ("Where is the bathroom?" "Where is the bank?" "Where is a restaurant?") and some emergency phrases ("Help me, please!" "I need a policeman!") in the native tongue of each of the countries you plan on visiting should be part of your vacation planning.
- ♦ In addition to knowing the language (however basic), invest in some current travel guides for the regions you'll be traveling through. Many travelers find that these books are the most important items they've packed.

Into the Wild

You're planning on leaving it all behind and forging your own honeymoon trail. If both of you are experienced with the outdoors, you're all set. However, if this is one of your first exploration trips, check and recheck to make sure you've planned for everything. Make sure you have your map (and any permits you may need—for your campsite, for example) before you hit the trail.

Don't stop at the sporting goods store on your way to the national park. Take the time to get acquainted with your equipment before you need to use it (think how frustrating it can be to pitch a tent in the dark), and plan for the worst possible weather. Make sure you have plenty of water and snacks, but don't overload yourself—your backpack shouldn't weigh more than twenty-five percent of your weight.

Hit Me Again!

Planning on turning your wedding jackpot into your first million? Not a sage plan. Give yourself a spending limit—allow yourself so much to gamble with, and know how much you're willing to lose before you set foot on the casino floor.

The hardest advice to follow is this: Quit while you're ahead. If you've had an amazing run of luck and you're starting to lose, walk away for a while. Get out of the casino, get your bearings, try to understand the value of the money in your hand while you've still got it. If you can win a little, you're way ahead of just about everyone else in that casino. In other words, don't think about how much more you could win by getting back to the table and doubling down. Take the money and run.

🅔🅓 Alert

Don't partake in the free alcohol most casinos offer. Here's a safe bet: If consuming alcohol in a casino were a sure-fire way for you to win, those drinks wouldn't be complimentary.

Long Trip or Short Trip?

If you're a teacher and you're planning a wedding for September, chances are you aren't going to have a lot of vacation time coming. On the other hand, any educator who chooses to honeymoon in June can look forward to weeks of rest and relaxation. Your work schedule (and vacation time) may likewise dictate the length of your honeymoon.

Postponing the Trip

Some couples choose not to take their honeymoon right after the wedding because of time or financial constraints. Is it all right to wait until the coast is clear (of work, of bills) to take that trip? Of course it is. The most important thing about your honeymoon is your state of mind. If vacationing right before the busiest time of your work year is going to put a damper on things, consider waiting until after things have settled down—your honeymoon will be a celebration of your marriage and a much-needed vacation.

Extended Honeymoons

Couples with great vacation benefits are planning honeymoons over an extended period of time. These trips can include world tours or summers at the beach. Think of the time you'll spend settling into life together, without a care in the world . . . .

If this sounds like something that might interest the two of you, consider three important points:

♦ Do you both have the vacation time, or will one of you have to quit your current job in order to take the time off?
♦ Do you have the cash to pay for an extended trip?
♦ Do both of you have the tolerance for life away from the comforts of home?

Obviously, if one of you is considering quitting work to take a long honeymoon, there are all sorts of factors to consider: Will you be able to find work upon returning home? If work is hard to come by, will you be in financial straits, or will you be secure for a while? Will taking the time off affect your career in the long run?

If you're thinking about traveling around the world for months on end, you should be able to finance it with money you've saved—not with your credit cards, and not with the money you're projecting you'll be receiving as wedding gifts.

The last question is of the utmost importance: If you hate sleeping in hotels, or if your fiancée is not a happy traveler, an extended trip—even though it's your honeymoon—could turn out to be a complete disaster. Keep it on the shorter side, and you'll come home still happily married.

 Fact

> For an idea of what an extended honeymoon *really* costs, talk to your travel agent—or, better yet, to someone who's actually traveled in the countries you're planning on visiting.

Weekend Flings

You can't always have it all. If you find that you'll have to delay the big expensive honeymoon indefinitely—because of work, or money, or both—don't sit pining away for the trip you'll take on your tenth anniversary. You only get to be newlyweds once, and the time is fleeting. Do your best to get away together, even if it's just for the weekend.

Why not book a room in the best hotel in town? Order room service, take advantage of their spa, take long walks together at sunset. It won't be cheap, but it's definitely less expensive than a world tour, and the time you'll spend bonding as man and wife will be priceless.

Honeymoon Help

Early on in the wedding budgeting, you and your fiancée established your priorities, and you decided that you would rather spend every penny you have on the wedding, and take a honeymoon when you can afford it. That's that. Or is it?

 Alert

> Be aware that you're probably going to end up covering some of the expenses of the trip yourself, so this is not the time to decide that the two of you will be needing every upgrade—when you scarcely have two nickels to rub together.

Nowadays, you can register for a honeymoon package with many travel agencies. You work with an agent to plan out your honeymoon and the cost of it; then you'll send announcements to your friends and family. Anyone who is so inclined can contribute to your honeymoon as a wedding gift. In fact, many travel agencies allow gift givers to contribute online. You're making gift-giving easy, they're giving you something you really want—everyone's thrilled!

Tourist Tips

You've seen the suckers in the papers and on the news—people who got ripped off in a foreign country and are in shock. You quietly scoff at their naiveté as you get into an odd-looking cab in a foreign country . . . and end up penniless on a back road in the middle of nowhere. How could you have avoided this?

At the Airport

Do your research on a foreign country before you go. Know the layout of the airport before you come off the jetway—have an idea of where the baggage claim is, where the taxi stand is, where the hotel shuttle should be. Don't allow locals to "assist" with your bags—unless you really want the help, that is. You'll end up tipping everyone left and right at best, and being the victim of a scam at worst.

Before you rent a car on your honeymoon, ask yourself if you really need one. Some foreign countries have very strict legal policies following accidents (i.e., you could end up in their jail). If you're visiting a big city, you'll have public transportation at your disposal, which will cost you far less than the cost of renting a car for a week. It's also very expensive to park a car in a city garage, and often impossible to find parking on the street.

Try to use the airport or hotel shuttle service to get to your resort. They're simply often the safest form of transportation.

Elsewhere

If your hotel room has a safe, use it. But be aware that if it's an electronic safe, insiders at certain hotels have been known to find ways to de-code your combination. Always wipe down the numbers with a damp cloth after you lock the safe so that your fingerprints can't be lifted off the numbers you've used.

Don't walk around carrying a map in your hand. You might as well take a permanent marker and write "Tourist" on your forehead. You'll be perceived as an easy mark by pickpockets and thieves.

 Essential

Change some of your money into the local currency before you leave, and never flash around large amounts of cash. Instead of putting your money in a wallet (or having your bride keep it in her purse), use a money belt. Sure, it looks like something your dad would wear, but it's a better way to hang on to your money.

Know the tipping customs where you are. For example, many European countries add the gratuity into your hotel and restaurant bill; this is also customary in many all-inclusive resorts. Unless you like throwing money around twice, you don't need to double-tip anyone.

Passports

Leaving the country? Not if your passport isn't up to date. Don't know the first thing about passports? Don't be intimidated. Getting one is relatively easy . . . if you don't have anything to hide, that is.

You can find the application itself (and loads of passport information) on the Department of State's Web site at *www.state.gov/travel*. If you're renewing a valid passport, you can apply by mail. If you've never had a passport; or if your passport has been lost, stolen, or damaged; or if you were under sixteen the last time you applied for one, you need to scoot yourself down to a passport agency or a passport acceptance facility to apply in person.

 Fact

You haven't the slightest idea of where to find a passport acceptance facility? You're worried that you'll have to travel many miles (and may actually need a passport) to locate one? You won't. If you live near a sizable post office, start your search there; you might also find one located in your county court or county offices.

What You'll Need

If your current passport has expired or you've never had a passport, you need to identify yourself when you submit your application. To this end, you'll need the following:

- **Proof of U.S. citizenship** (your original birth certificate, naturalization certificate, or previous passport).
- **Proof of identification.** This can include a valid driver's license or military ID.
- **Two passport photos.** These can be taken at many one-hour photo shops. There are regulations as to the size (2" x 2") and the content (you must be facing forward, for example—no mug shots allowed).
- **Fee.** Currently, the fee totals $85.

When Should You Apply?

Generally speaking, passports take about six weeks to find their way into your hands. Give yourself at least three months to allow for any glitches—and more time than that, if you have it, just to be on the safe side.

There are Web sites that promise to aid you in obtaining your passport much faster than the standard six weeks it takes for mere mortals to receive theirs (the expedited times range from twenty-four hours to several weeks). Since you won't wait till the last minute to get the passport ball rolling (will you?), you probably won't need to look into these services. If you want your passport *right now*, though, you should know that a hefty fee is included (a couple of hundred dollars for the fastest service).

Perfection Guaranteed?

Really, the best advice anyone can give you about your honeymoon consists of three steps: Plan early; do your homework; and then . . . relax.

Just because it's your honeymoon does not mean that the planets are required to line up and guarantee you a perfect vacation. Every trip has its ups and downs; you may feel pressured to make this the ultimate vacation, complete with romance, adventure, great food, unbelievable sights, and perfect conversation. It could happen.

Sometimes life takes its own course, though, and the same problems that find their way into everyday life plague honeymooners. Take, for example, Raj. On his honeymoon in Spain, he was injured in a scooter accident. Spent some time in the hospital with his new bride by his side—and was then confined to a wheelchair. Suffice it to say that the newlyweds grew very close on this trip. He was dependant on his wife for the smallest things, of course, but he made it up to her by summoning the strength to have a little fun in some nightclubs, hobbling around instead of boogying.

Was their honeymoon special in spite of—or maybe even because of—these unusual circumstances? Yes, it was.

Deborah's husband managed to injure himself in the days before their wedding and was forced to start the honeymoon with stitches in his shin. Did Deborah cry foul because *she* had to remove the stitches during her honeymoon? No, she did not. She rolled with the punches.

You and your bride might find yourselves struggling to make yourselves understood in a foreign country where seemingly no one speaks English; or you might be delayed by an airline's mechanical troubles or the weather; one of you could be so exhausted from the wedding and the travel that a week-long nap sounds like the ideal honeymoon.

Don't give in to the pressure of having the Perfect Honeymoon. Perfection is all about *your* definition of the word— and no one else's. Enjoy each other, allow yourselves to act a little giddy about the fact that you're Mr. and Mrs., and let the rest take care of itself.

CHAPTER 9

Bachelor Party

The funny thing about the phrase *bachelor party* is that when you hear it, your adrenaline starts pumping, and you love your friends right now for planning this for you—even though it's months before the actual event. Meanwhile, when your fiancée hears the same phrase, she gets sick to her stomach and fights back her tears. Bachelor parties have a definite reputation for courting trouble, and for causing trouble. How can you get through the bachelor party and face yourself in the mirror the next morning? Very carefully.

The Balancing Act

You want the typical bachelor party. Your bride wants you to behave yourself. You know these two desires are completely incompatible—so do you choose what you want or what she wants? Or do you take the easy road, and do what you want and lie about it? Hard choices for a groom to make. A little advice follows.

She's Not Stupid

Of course you know your fiancée is more than a pretty face. She is well aware of:

- What goes on at bachelor parties.
- What your friends are planning.
- What you're planning.
- That little twitch under your eye when you're lying.

 Fact

What she's going to be looking for is assurance from you that certain lines will not be crossed during your bachelor party. These will vary from relationship to relationship —so don't expect that you'll be given the same carte blanche that your best friend was given by his fiancée.

Since your friends will probably keep a big part of the night a secret from you (to keep your bride from catching wind of their big plans, if nothing else), and since they will most likely swear you—and each other—to secrecy on the night of the big party, is there any way for you to be one hundred percent honest with your fiancée—and should you be? Aren't there unspoken privacy rules concerning the bachelor party?

 Essential

If your fiancée is good enough to you to overlook something that would normally upset her—like a stripper—so that you can have a wild bachelor party, be good enough to her to respect her ultimate wishes.

Well, you might be in for a surprise. Your bride may not want to know every single detail of the evening. After all, she has her own bachelorette party in the works, and she'll have a thing or two that she's going to keep to herself, as well.

Some women have no problem with their men visiting "gentlemen's clubs"—other women have huge issues with these places. Whatever her particular take on the issue, the vast majority of women will put it aside for this one evening because this is simply what most men do at bachelor parties. The line may be drawn there: You can go, but you can't touch. The line may be a little further south: You can stuff money in the back of a stripper's g-string, but not in the front.

The Mole

The oath of secrecy is popular with men at bachelor parties. And that oath can seem ironclad at two in the morning when you've consumed the better part of a bottle of whiskey.

Be aware that secrets often find their way out of the closet—usually when you least expect it. And the strong silent pal who boogied with you and five hookers on the night of your bachelor party might just be the one who has the most to say later on, when he reveals to your bride that he's been in love with her for years and he would never consent to a bachelor party like the one you had if she were to marry him. Be forewarned: Everyone has an agenda and nothing stays a secret forever.

Planning

Way back when, bachelor parties were held the night before the wedding. Why, you ask? You're just going to knock back a few brews with the boys . . . or so you think. Little do you know what the boys have planned for you.

When

Do not let your pals talk you into going out with them the night before the wedding. Do not leave the rehearsal dinner to go down to the corner bar with them; don't tell your bride that you're all going to the movies. Your intentions may be pure enough, but there's bound to be one pal in the bunch who wants to see you completely trashed on the eve of your wedding. For him, it's sport. You're just the prey.

Why

Why? Why, you ask, *can't* you go out with the boys for one last hurrah the night before you say, "I do"?

There are so many reasons. The biggest two are because your bride has spent years dreaming of this day; and the two of you have spent many months and many dollars planning the Perfect Wedding. If you dare to show up at the church incoherent, nauseated, and shaking so badly from the effects of all those shots you drank the night before, your bride will kill you. (This is not an exaggeration—she may literally try to take your life, or at the very least, she may make you wish that she *would* end it.)

 Fact

Ideally, your bachelor party should take place at least a week before the wedding—two to four weeks before the big day is better still. The date will be close enough to the wedding so that you'll be caught up in the moment, and yet far enough away that you'll be able to recover from the inevitable hangover that you swore you wouldn't have.

The bride, however, will only be the first in a long line of Groom Haters on your wedding day should you choose to stagger toward the altar with the scent of booze hanging around you like a skunk's odor. The bride's mother and father will be livid; the preacher won't hide his disgust (and could actually postpone the nuptials if there's any doubt as to your ability to consent to the marriage); bridesmaids will curse you; and from there, various guests will line up to tell you how immature and irresponsible you are.

Or, more likely, they'll tell each other, and you'll go down in family history as "Susie's Jerk Husband—the one who showed up drunk at the church, remember?"

Where?

Anywhere, really. Though big bachelor parties are often held in bars or in rented halls, you can have a smaller party at a friend's house. Another popular option is to put the party on wheels. Renting a limo for the night kills two birds with one stone: Your transportation is taken care of, and the party is wherever the men decide to take it.

If you're planning on bringing the party to a restaurant, call ahead and check with the management to make sure they can accommodate (and will welcome) your entire group.

Alert

This is not the time for you to steal the show with your drunken exploits. You'll be meeting many members of the bride's family for the first time—think about that first impression. Do you want to seem charming, sophisticated, and deserving of this beautiful woman? Or do you want to act like a frat pledge in a tux?

Another idea, if your party is on the small side, is to rent a suite in a posh hotel—you can spend your pre- and post-party hours there, or you can spend the entire evening. Just keep in mind that you men are not, in fact, rock stars, and trashing a luxurious hotel room is a very costly mistake—one that you won't make twice.

What?

If you're a novice at this bachelor party thing, you might wonder what all the fuss is about. Geez Louise, can't a few guys get together before a wedding and pass some time without risking their reputations? Hmm . . . no.

Even if you've never been to a bachelor party, your friends have. And if they haven't, they'll be looking for information—in books, on the Internet, from other friends. They're going to be left with the idea that all bachelor parties must include:

- **Strippers.** Many, many strippers, in fact.
- **Drinking.** To the point of unconsciousness.
- **Gambling.** Poker in the basement, or a trip to the casino, or betting on who throws up first.
- **Pornographic materials.** In the form of blow-up dolls, magazines, movies, etc.
- **Humiliating the groom.** That's you, Guy. Read the items on this list again and use your imagination.

Not your bag? Speak up now—or go along for the ride. Contrary to popular opinion, your bachelor party does not have to take place in a bar or in a topless dance club. In that same vein, your bachelor party does not have to follow the standard formula of drinking to excess and watching topless dancers for hours on end. It's your party; if you don't like the direction the planning is taking, do some planning of your own. The end of this chapter has some ideas for alternatives to the traditional stag.

The "In" Crowd

You're not planning the bachelor party, so why should you be worried about the guest list? Picture oil and water. They won't mix no matter what you do. Now picture the oil that is your bachelor party and these watery guests are floating around:

Your Boss

Oh, my. Your buttoned-up boss is over in the corner of the bar trying like mad to escape the stripper who has seemingly zeroed in on his big fat wallet. He's looking like he'd like to vaporize, and you're wondering what this means for your quarterly employee review coming up.

 Fact

Rule of thumb: Rowdy bachelor parties and business don't mix—for many reasons—and this extends to coworkers and clients, as well as your boss. If your relationship has never made the foray into the world of nightclubs and whooping it up together, this is not the occasion to open that can of worms.

Your friends are going to egg you on all night long, and it's probably fair to say that you're going to let loose more than you normally would. If your boss, coworkers, or clients have never seen you outside the confines of your office, they could come away completely shell-shocked and wondering about your character.

Think of the awkward moment when you face your coworkers Monday morning and no one dares to mention the stripper-and-whipped-cream incident. In fact, no one will look you in the face. Better to leave them out of this particular event, even if you're inviting them to the wedding. You will presumably resemble your professional self a little more at the ceremony and reception than you will at your bachelor party.

The Bride's Family

Don't be surprised if your bride's brothers and father show up at your bachelor party. Chances are they're going to be invited, so in the name of preventing decades of questionable glances thrown your way during Sunday dinners, you might want to discuss the entertainment with whoever is planning the party beforehand.

🔴 Alert

Should you be judged by the bachelor party your friends throw for you? Probably not. Will you be? Probably—depending on your eagerness to participate in the free-for-all. If you're socializing with the guests, you're going to present a better picture than if you're sitting on a stripper's lap.

Take Deborah's story—and learn from it: "My husband's brother threw him a stag party a couple of months before our wedding. My dad and brother as well as my husband's father, uncles, and other family members were present. My brother-in-law hired strippers to perform at a bar they rented out. These weren't your average

take-your-shirt-off-and-shake 'em strippers. They were
lesbian strippers. And they were apparently very unin-
hibited. Anything you can imagine went on between the
strippers that evening."

Enough to make you a little uncomfortable? It should
be. Some older folks will laugh this type of thing off, attrib-
uting it to the Sexual Revolution and this new generation
(X? Y?), but some won't.

And this is the very type of thing that can create tension
between you and your future father-in-law for months (if
not years), when he starts to wonder why he gave you his
blessing to marry his innocent daughter.

Two, Two, Two Parties in One

If you're in a situation where you feel obligated to invite
conservative family members and/or business associates,
plan a two-part party. Meet the group for dinner or drinks—
make it something with a definite ending point. Once this
early get-together ends, you and the rowdy boys can continue on with the real bachelor party.

Fun Is a Funny Word

Fun can mean so many different things, depending on your
outlook. Bachelor parties are supposed to be all about cutting loose and having a good time. But there's a difference
between having fun and crossing the line into questionable
territory. You're walking on thin ice, whether you realize it
or not. Proceed cautiously.

Fun vs. Making the Bride Cry

Know your bride; know what she will tolerate and what she won't. If you're engaged to an incredibly open-minded woman who loves experimentation, you're in a very different boat from the guy who's engaged to a conservative woman. Your fiancée is not going to change her colors simply because you're off to your bachelor party. You're her now and forever man, and she has certain expectations of you.

If you're engaged to a girl who's on the more reserved side (i.e., she doesn't like strip clubs and she isn't thrilled with the idea of your being out-of-your-mind drunk), think carefully about your bachelor party, your expectations of the event, and how it could affect your relationship with her. Some women are very opposed to the traditional bachelor party, as they feel it's antimarriage. If your own bride-to-be feels this way, you're going to need to watch your step so that you're still engaged the morning after the big shindig.

 **Essential**

No one is suggesting that your bachelor party should be scaled back to the point of sitting home with the guys, reading passages from Shakespeare to each other. Just take the time to evaluate whether the level of rowdiness that your friends have planned for you is worth the trouble it may cause with your fiancée.

How can you accomplish this? For starters, you need to trust the guys who are planning your bachelor party. If your wild brother is in charge and he has a penchant for loose women and illegal activities, think again before you agree to put yourself in his hands for the night.

If your pals keep telling you that the whole night is a big surprise—and you're going to love it—be a little leery. Chances are they know how your bride feels about the whole event. That doesn't mean they're going to respect her feelings. Believe it or not, sometimes friends really resent the appearance of a girlfriend or wife in the picture, and they'll do anything to come between the two of you.

Worst-case scenario (for you, anyway): You find yourself somewhere you know you shouldn't be. Maybe you're sitting in the middle of a strip joint and there's a scantily-clothed woman dancing on your lap. (You get the picture.) You have two choices: stay and revel in the fun (and remember, that word has different meanings—your bride won't accept the excuse that you were just having "fun"); or leave, and risk being called a wet blanket.

You know the right thing to do (as you hear your fiancée's words, "No strippers!" echoing in your head) is to leave, but the fun thing is to stay. You're a grownup. You have to make this call on your own. Chances are if you're three sheets to the wind, you're not going anywhere, and if you're sober . . . you might. Just remember this: The bachelor party is supposed to be fun. It's not supposed to end your relationship.

Walking the Line

How are you supposed to know what's acceptable behavior and what's going to leave you stranded in the dog-house? Turn the tables for a minute.

Look at your bride. She's beautiful, she's smart, she has a great sense of humor . . . she's a real catch, and any man would be lucky to have her, right? In fact, sometimes you can't believe she agreed to marry you.

Now picture her engaging in the same activities that you have in mind for your bachelor party. (That mental picture you have of her at her bachelorette party, stuffing dollar bills into some guy's g-string—using her teeth, no less—isn't such a pleasant image, you say?) Life isn't about keeping score, of course, and/or one-upping each other. But in this case . . . maybe it's the best way to judge what's acceptable and what's not.

Talk It Out

Some grooms avoid discussing the bachelor party with their fiancées precisely because they'd rather not know where the line in the sand is drawn—because if you never hear your girlfriend say that she disapproves of certain activities, you can't be held accountable for taking part in those activities, right?

Wrong. Since you are preparing to walk down the aisle soon, you probably have a pretty good idea of where your fiancée stands on certain issues, like excessive alcohol consumption and strippers. By pleading ignorance after the fact, you'll only be digging yourself in deeper. She's not going to buy that excuse, for starters, and she may begin to question why she's marrying a man who doesn't have a clue about her feelings.

Keep in mind that your fiancée is running on emotional steam in the weeks preceding the wedding, and any inappropriate behavior will be under the microscope at this point in the engagement, as she wonders if she even knows you and if you intend to behave this way after the wedding.

 Alert

If you're truly in the dark as to what's acceptable as far as your bride-to-be is concerned—she's a real partier, for instance, but she balks at your having more than one beer—address the issues before your bachelor party.

Setting Limits

Now that you and the bride have either laid things out on the table or you've accepted that there are just certain things you're not going to get away with, even at your own bachelor party, how are you going to get through this event without getting in trouble?

Easy. You're a big boy. Set your own margins for the evening, and stay in control of your faculties.

- Know how much alcohol you can drink without falling over. In other words, don't accept shot after shot after beer after beer.
- Other women? Off limits, babe—with the possible exception of tipping a dancer.
- Have an alternative method of transportation—like a cab—in mind. Don't depend on your wild friends

to take you home when you've had enough. You're stranded with them until you've proved you can still party like a single guy.

Not the night you had in mind? Picture these two very different mornings-after: The first one with you being able to remember exactly how you got home, and everything that happened the night before; the other one with you waking up in some dude's apartment, reeking of something foul (is it you or the apartment?), and knowing that you'll have some explaining to do when you find your way back to your fiancée, who will be waiting.

Groomsmen or Scapegoats?

Your friends are the greatest. They've planned an unbelievable bachelor party for you. It's going to be out of control, and since it's your last hurrah as a single guy, you deserve it. Besides, you can blame them for anything your fiancée gets mad about. You've got life by the tail, don't you?

Owning Up

Coming home inebriated from your bachelor party is probably the least your bride is expecting. Don't try to tell her your friends poured the alcohol down your throat. Don't tell her you weren't smoking when it's clear that you were. And don't tell her that you didn't have any fun at all without her. She's going to wonder what else you're lying about.

Scapegoats Serve a Limited Purpose

Your bride is going to hold you accountable for certain behaviors, whether you try to place the blame on your friends, and whether your friends try to tell her it was their fault. If you come home from your bachelor party covered in hickies, you can pretty much forget shifting the blame. That's all on you.

It's not the worst thing in the world to blame your pals for the excessive drinking; it may even be true to some extent. And the fact that you were unable to leave the strip joint until the dawn started breaking—because the other guys refused to go—might also be mostly true.

Blaming your friends for the fact that you had your hands all over another woman at your bachelor party isn't going to fly with your fiancée (if she catches wind of it—which she will). This might be something your friends have all done; maybe it's commonplace in your family. It shouldn't be, and if your bachelor party dreams are all wrapped up in visions of one last conquest, you probably shouldn't be getting married.

Alternatives to the Traditional Stag

You don't want to upset your fiancée with the bachelor party, which she's been crying over for a month now. Or maybe you just don't feel comfortable with the whole idea—you've never been a bar-goer, and you're not a drinker. If you're looking for something that suits your personality a little better than the traditional beer-and-stripper stag, consider an alternative night on the town.

Coed Bachelor/ette Party

Sometimes it just doesn't make sense for the bride and groom and all of their friends and relatives to split into separate camps for single-sex parties. The bride may have a number of close male friends, while your close relationships might predominantly include females—friends, sisters, cousins. A coed party is a great way to get these groups together and mingling before the wedding, and in a way that's far more comfortable than bringing random guests together based on their gender.

 Fact

If you and the bride decide a coed party is a better option for you and your friends, let it be known early on, before your friends start planning separate parties for each of you. The two of you can either take on the planning yourselves, or you can help your respective friends out with the initial planning stages and let them co-plan the evening from there.

For example, if your fiancée's best friend is a man, how comfortable is he really going to be at your bachelor party, with your friends and your family? Likewise, if you and your sister are very close, wouldn't she rather be included in a party with you than spend an evening making small talk with the bride's friends?

Another reason to think about a coed party is to get the wedding party talking—before the wedding. If you and your bride have two completely different sets of friends—

people who are complete strangers to one another—you might be a little concerned about how everyone is going to get along when you pair them up and send them down the aisle together. Give them a chance to really get to know each other beforehand.

Sporty Groom

You're into the golf scene or the outdoors. So why not plan a bachelor outing instead of the traditional night in a tavern?

Grab the guys and play a round of golf. Celebrate afterward with steaks and a round of drinks in the clubhouse. Fishing's your sport? Make a weekend of it. Rent a cabin on the lake and invite your closest friends. If hiking is your thing, race each other to the top of the mountain and toast your impending marriage at the summit. You can turn any hobby or sport into a bachelor outing or an entire weekend. Consider what you could make of these guys-only vacations:

- Skiing
- Hunting
- Snowmobiling
- Scuba diving
- Camping
- Skydiving

A lot of men find trips with their buddies far more appealing than spending the night in a loud club trying to be heard over the music and commotion. And it's virtually impossible to get in trouble with a stripper while climbing a mountain in the heat of the day (*virtually* impossible).

CHAPTER 10

Super Groom's Final Checklist

Y ou've been through the wedding planning wringer at this point. You're not sure what you've done, but you know it has been plenty. With the final days drawing nearer, you need to go over the things that absolutely, positively must be done in order to secure a happy future with your bride. Some of this will sound like familiar stuff; other things might set off an alarm bell in your head (as though you knew you were forgetting something).

Preparations for the Ceremony

If only getting married were as uncomplicated as many grooms wish it were: Two people would show up at the Justice of the Peace and say, "I do." There wouldn't be much fuss beyond that. However, weddings in this day and age—as you well know by this point—are far more involved, and it's every groom for himself. Make sure you're not the guy who shows up at the altar in a T-shirt because you didn't check your tux bag to make sure your wing-tipped-collared shirt was in there.

The Legalities

Have you applied for the marriage license? If not, get your tail in gear and get down to your county clerk's office, pronto. Some states require that both of you apply in person for the license; other states require one of you. Remember to bring cash (many localities will not accept checks or credit cards) and if you live in one of the few states that still require a blood test (the vast majority have done away with it), be prepared for that, also. Don't lose the license once it's in your possession.

Don't forget to bring the license to the rehearsal or the wedding. (Whichever event your officiant prefers.) This is your proof that both of you are legally willing and able to be married, and without it . . . you're up a creek. After it's been signed by the officiant and your witnesses, it will be sent back to the county clerk to be recorded. You are now officially husband and wife, in the eyes of your state.

Alert

You must have the license in hand for your officiant to sign (along with a witness or two in most states); though the officiant is supposed to sign it after the ceremony, ask him if he'd like you to bring the license to the rehearsal (when there's less chance of it being lost in the shuffle).

Your Tux

The week before your wedding, pop into the tux shop and double-check that they have the right information on file. Don't take an employee's word for it; ask him or her to point out to *you* which tux they have you down for (hopefully, you'll remember which one you chose), and how many they'll have ready for pickup.

 Essential

When you arrive for the tux pickup, try on the entire outfit—accessories and all. If you have no idea how to wear something (or how to tie your bow tie), ask. This is part of the service.

If you're planning on having six guys wear tuxedos and the shop only has five in their computer, something's amiss. They've either misplaced someone's measurements or one of your pals hasn't been measured yet. (What he's waiting for is anyone's guess.) Don't fret—yet. This is exactly the reason why you're doing this last-minute check.

Unfortunately, you'll probably be instructed to pick up your tux the night before the wedding—or possibly two nights before. This doesn't do much for alleviating your stress; a groom's gotta do what a groom's gotta do.

Even though the tux shop might be in a total frenzy (especially if you're getting married in the summer months—you'll be competing for space with a bevy of other grooms), remember that the tux shop employees are there for you—even if they don't seem particularly happy about it at the moment.

In summary:

♦ **Don't wait until the last minute.** If you can pick up your tux two days before the wedding, do it. If there are any problems (missing accessories, alterations), you're giving the shop ample time to fix them.

♦ **Try on the tux, the tie, the vest, the shoes.** When you leave, make sure you have everything.

♦ **Encourage your groomsmen to follow your lead in trying on their ensembles.** Make sure your linebacker brother isn't trying to squeeze himself into a pair of high-water pants.

♦ **If alterations are necessary, don't sweat it too much.** Hopefully you've chosen a shop with a tailor on duty, and minor repairs are a snap for these professionals.

♦ **If something feels (or looks) too loose or too tight, speak up.** You don't want your pants falling down when you're dancing with your new mother-in-law.

♦ **Make sure you know when the tuxes must be returned.**
The fee for renting them an extra day is something you
and your men want to avoid.

This is also a good time to touch base with your best
man (or your brother, or whomever you trust with the
task) and arrange to have him return your tux for you,
as you will be busy doing other things the morning after
your wedding.

 Alert

This isn't the time to try out a new cut or color. Go with
the old tried-and-true or else you regret the decision
for the rest of your life—or at least every time you
look at your wedding pictures.

Your (Tee Hee) Grooming

Everyone knows that you shouldn't get a haircut the day
before a big event—and especially not on the day before
your wedding. You know how long it takes your hair to
settle down before it gets in its groove—for most men, it's
about two weeks between the cut and the *look*.

If you want to go all-out and try a manicure or pedicure,
this is as good a time as any to treat yourself to one or both.
Beware trying out a new facial scrub or mask-type treatment in the days before the wedding, though; a bad reaction could leave you swollen and embarrassed.

The Rehearsal

Everyone's chitchatting in their places, the priest is in his street clothes, your nephew is running willy-nilly through the church . . . what kind of rehearsal *is* this? This isn't the wedding you've planned and imagined. Will things be so casual and disorganized tomorrow?! No. Think of this as a relaxed run-through. When tomorrow comes, you'll be able to feel the excitement in the air.

At the Church

Most churches have a scheduled time for rehearsals. What happens during your block of time? A mock wedding, basically. If you have a wedding consultant or if the church has a wedding coordinator (many larger churches do, just to keep things moving along as they should—and your paid coordinator may have to defer to any rules the church has), she will instruct the bridesmaids on where to stand, how slowly they should proceed down the aisle, whether or not they'll be escorted by a groomsman—that sort of thing.

She will do the same for everyone who has a part to play—your mother, your mother-law, your groomsmen, anyone who's reading during the ceremony (or bringing gifts to the altar). She'll have special instructions for the maid of honor and the best man, and most especially for your bride. (And by the way, if your church doesn't have a coordinator, and you haven't hired a planner, your minister will lead you through the rehearsal.)

You'll stand at the altar in the now eerily quiet church and watch as your bride and her father walk toward you.

She'll be wearing a dress you've seen a hundred times before and you'll be moved to the point of . . . not tears, exactly. But this is when it will hit you: You're getting married the next day, and you'll wish tomorrow were right now.

 Fact

You may give the priest the marriage license at this point; now's also the perfect time to take care of any fees associated with the church, so that you won't have to worry about it tomorrow.

So, you'll run through the ceremony in its shortened form—how the exchange of rings will go, who should be doing what (the maid of honor will take the bride's flowers and straighten her train, for example). Before you know it, you've been fake-married by your own priest, and you're out the door.

Nowhere to Rehearse?

If you're going to say your vows in a restaurant or a banquet facility that's swamped with other ceremonies, you may not have access to the location the night (or even several nights) before the ceremony. Are you to show up at the ceremony without knowing where you'll stand and just play things by ear?

Nah. Take matters into your own hands and get creative. Host your rehearsal dinner somewhere where you and your almost-bride will be able to put everyone in their places, so to speak.

Having everyone to your home is a good idea. You can lay out the area for your attendants, discuss the floor plan of your wedding site, and take charge of your own run-through of the ceremony.

Things you shouldn't overlook:

♦ Will the groomsmen escort the bridesmaids down the aisle, or meet them halfway? Partner your attendants up now, so no one is confused as to whom they should be walking with the following day.

♦ When should the first bridesmaid begin her trek down the aisle, and how slowly should she walk?

♦ Upon arriving at the aisle, where should the attendants stand/sit? Will all of them stay at the altar, or will only your honor attendants remain at your sides? Will the best man be holding the rings? The maid of honor should prepare herself now for her special duties (holding the bride's flowers and fixing her dress).

♦ It's customary for the bride and groom to leave the altar first, followed by their attendants in pairs. Do a run-through of this, too, so that your best man and maid of honor don't jump the gun and steal your thunder.

Rub-a-Dub-Dub, Where's the Grub?

You'll invite the wedding party, their significant others, immediate family members, your officiant, and his or her spouse. If you want to extend an invitation to out-of-town guests, they'll surely appreciate your thoughtfulness.

Remember, this is your gig. You are not bound by any sort of wedding covenant to host an elaborate affair, though that's perfectly acceptable. Your rehearsal dinner can be a cookout or a pizza party; it can be a sit-down affair in a nice restaurant or a catered event in your aunt's spacious backyard.

 **Question**

What are your duties during the dinner?
Play the host as well as you can. You may feel that your nerves are finally getting the better of you, or you may feel preternaturally calm. You can't predict your emotions before the day arrives. Don't drink too much, and don't follow your guy friends to the tavern tonight. You need your beauty sleep, you know.

This is the time for you and your bride to present your gifts to your attendants and your mothers (and whomever else you're feeling particularly generous toward).

Wedding Gift for Your Honey

Chapter 4 gave you some ideas for a wedding gift for your new wife. Many grooms give their bride this gift at the rehearsal or even on the wedding day itself. If your bride is holding herself together fairly well, this might work out swell for you. If, on the other hand, she's freaking out in the days before the wedding, you might just want to hold on to that gift until she can focus on the meaning behind it. Following are a few words of wisdom concerning the bride's potentially precarious emotional state on the eve of your nuptials.

Doesn't She Like It?

One groom gave his fiancée a music box in the shape of a sewing basket the night before their wedding. His fiancée didn't fuss over it the way he thought she might, and in fact, he recalls, "She didn't even want to show it to anyone. When her friends looked at it, she kind of just pushed it aside. It was pretty clear that she didn't like it."

What would this groom have done differently? "I was trying to surprise her," he says, "and she's usually really happy with anything I give her. I think this was such a big occasion, she was expecting something else—something more substantial, like earrings or a necklace or something along those lines—and that's so unlike her, I didn't even stop to think that that might be the case."

Another bride was completely thrown at her rehearsal dinner when her groom presented her with a diamond tennis bracelet—after they had both agreed not to buy each other gifts. She says, "We had spent so much money on the wedding and the honeymoon that we had to draw the line somewhere. And honestly, I didn't need the bracelet. I love it, of course, but you know, I was planning on putting that money toward a *car*. I didn't know how to react to this gift. I was touched, on the one hand, and on the other hand, I was furious that he had made this huge purchase without discussing it with me—and I didn't have a gift for him, which made it even worse."

She's Crying

Remember: The closer the ceremony, the less stable your bride's emotional state may be. The groom who gave his wife the music box later asked her why she hated it, and she burst into tears. Turns out she had been on the verge of breaking down for days, as she battled with the dressmaker, who only that morning had put the final touches on the bride's gown, and the priest, who had not-so-kindly made some last-minute changes to the ceremony. This bride was in no condition to graciously accept her groom's gift—she would have reacted the same way to a pair of ruby earrings or a mop.

In other words, it wasn't that his choice of a gift was poor—she just couldn't handle *anything* else at that point. Sounds silly to most grooms, until they find themselves in a similar situation with their own soon-to-be-wives.

 Alert

If the bride is just completely out of control during the rehearsal, consider waiting until your honeymoon before bestowing your gift on her. She'll appreciate it more when she's back in this planet's orbit.

Choosing a Gift

When you choose a gift for your bride, take time to think about what this whole event means to her, and what *she* might like. If she's a very whimsical woman, for example, look for a gift that's going to suit her tastes—like a signed original painting from her favorite local artist. If she's very traditional, you might want to buy her something that can be engraved with her new initials.

Beware the temptation to make things easy on yourself simply by spending a lot of money on a gift. That money is going right down the drain if you're not considering her wants and needs. For example, if she doesn't ever wear a watch, you should probably skip the jewel-encrusted timepiece you've been eyeing for her. Beautiful? Yes, it is. But she'll take one look at it and wonder how you could not know—after being with her for all this time—that she doesn't believe in wearing a watch, and she will be irritated with you for blowing all that cash on a gift that's useless to her.

Likewise, if you've made a deal not to buy gifts for each other—or not to spend a bundle on gifts—*honor that agreement*. This is no time to play Russian Roulette with the bank account or your bride's emotions.

Wedding Eve

You've picked up your tux, you've practiced the ceremony, you've had the rehearsal dinner . . . now what? You know it's not a good idea to get loaded on the night before your wedding, even if you're feeling extremely nervous—or giddy. Still, you've got eighteen hours to fill between now and the ceremony.

Take the time to touch base with your fiancée tonight. As the wedding countdown draws to a close, the two of you may find that you've been so crazy busy, you've hardly had time to speak to each other. Now's the time to make sure both of you are completely *physically* prepared for the big day, and for the honeymoon. For example, has she gone to the drugstore and picked up all of her necessities? Have you? Time's a-wastin'. Before you know it, you'll be on the plane to Hawaii, you'll remember that you're out of contact solution, and you'll curse yourself.

 Essential

Above all, savor this moment—the anticipation, the excitement, the nervousness. Soon all of this will be a memory, and life will settle into routine. You'll forget how insane things seemed right before the wedding and you'll choose to remember how eager you were to get to the church on time.

If your bride has the jitters, there may not be much that you can do to settle her down. Some brides lose it in a fit of tears and nervous energy the night before the wedding. Even if you can't stop her emotional roller-coaster ride, you can offer her your support and remind her that you can't wait to be her husband. Sometimes just being there is all you need to do.

Make some memories now—hold hands, talk about the future, or just cuddle up and sit quietly. Tomorrow (and tomorrow and tomorrow) is waiting for you.

Honeymoon

It was hard work, but you planned the perfect honeymoon. It's two in the morning, you're getting married at noon, and you can't find the plane tickets. Or your passport. Your new wife's first order of business is going to be to sell you on the black market. Not really—because you won't put yourself in this position (will you?).

Guard Your Paperwork

In order to avoid standing in line at the airport until your first anniversary, you will most likely receive your boarding passes prior to your day of travel. Do not throw them on the coffee table with your sports magazines. Don't put them in the glove compartment along with every receipt and gum wrapper you've collected in the past eighteen months.

If you have a fire-safe box or a safe, put your tickets safely within their confines. If not, find a spot for them—a place that won't slip your mind. If your top dresser drawer is that spot, fine. If it's the filing cabinet in your home office, great.

 Essential

Don't forget: This is an out-of-town vacation, not a brief pit stop after the wedding. You'll need to make the usual vacation arrangements: Pet/house sitter, mail/paper stopped, timers on, etc.

When you are packing for your honeymoon, don't forget the tickets. This is your responsibility, and though it sounds obvious enough to you right now, you're going to be a busy bee in the days before your wedding. Because most men don't consider packing for a trip a priority, you may find yourself packing only a day or two (or, if you're like a lot of men, perhaps just hours) before your wedding. There's inherent danger in this plan, as your last-minute packing may become distracted by a call from the bride, or the tux shop, or your best man, resulting in you forgetting your swim trunks on your bed—along with your plane tickets.

Tickets shouldn't be packed in the bottom of your suitcase, of course, because you'll need them at the airport. They're better off in your carry-on bag, along with all of your other valuables and can't-live-without items.

Even if you are completely against the idea of carry-on luggage (you just despise those people who are always trying to squeeze their bags into overhead compartments), pack a carry-on bag anyway. If your luggage is temporarily waylaid (your suitcase goes to Munich while you're vacationing in Miami), you'll be very happy to have a pair of clean underwear and deodorant at your disposal (as well as prescription medicines, your glasses—and anything else you absolutely can't do without).

Hotel Reservations

If you're staying in a local hotel on your wedding night and/or on your honeymoon, confirm your reservations before you show up on their doorstep. When the reservations were made, you should have been given a confirmation number. If you lost it, you'll have to give your information all over again, but otherwise, don't panic.

When confirming your reservations, ask about:

♦ The room size
♦ The nightly rate
♦ Smoking/nonsmoking rooms
♦ Check-in time

If this information does not match up to your original criteria, ask to speak to the manager on duty. Don't shrug off a price increase; don't accept their word that the "new" check-in time is now five in the evening. If this is not what you were told when you reserved the room, straighten it out now.

 Fact

Don't forget: Your bride's tickets should be booked in her maiden name in accordance with airline and airport security policies. You'll both need a valid photo ID in order to board your flight.

Also, call to confirm your airline reservations at least twenty-four hours in advance. Since check-in times for domestic and international flights change with the security policies in airports, check the current recommendations on the day before your flight, as well. (The check-in times vary according to whether you're checking bags or not.) These tasks can be completed by calling your airline's automated check-in/reservations telephone number. Quick, easy, all done.

Surprise!

A bride who loves surprises may just trust you to plan a surprise honeymoon. In this case, she'll be on a need-to-know agenda. Don't forget to tell her if she needs to update her passport, for example, as a stern, unyielding customs agent is not the surprise she'll be looking for on her honeymoon.

And don't pull the old Surprise Switcheroo on her unless you're one hundred percent sure that it will only add to her delight, keeping in mind that she's been dealing with all sorts of vendors and family members and she might be on edge. In other words, if she's going to need a swimsuit, don't tell her to pack her snow gear. You might find yourself zipped up and trapped in her parka while she combs the beaches by herself.

Got the Cash?

Even if the two of you have agreed to charge the bulk of your honeymoon expenses (so that you won't risk carrying—and losing—large amounts of cash), you should have some cold hard currency on your person for emergencies. You never know when a connecting flight will be canceled, for instance. You could find yourself in some strange hotel overnight, next door to the one restaurant in the area—which operates on a cash-only basis.

Cash also comes in handy for little things along the way, like the toothpaste and shampoo that neither of you remembered to pack.

And speaking of which . . . budgeting for the honeymoon often includes the cost of travel, food, souvenirs, sightseeing, and the like. If you're headed to a tourist hot-spot, pack all of your necessities, like your toiletries and medicines, before you leave home. Sure, you may feel like your parents on a road trip, but your parents pack this way for a reason—it saves them a lot of dough.

When you're in an unfamiliar area and you're desperate for allergy medicine, you don't know which places are reasonably priced and which are known for outrageously gouging tourists. Even in the town you live in, you have your preferences based on price. Since you're not going to spend your honeymoon comparison shopping, you'll be forced to use the nearest stores—and the stores that are near vacation spots are there to make a buck off of *you*.

 Essential

Consider carrying at least a couple of hundred dollars in cash and splitting the amount between the two of you, so that in the event that you do lose a few bills along the way, you've got another stash at the ready.

Obviously, buying one package of antihistamine isn't going to break your bank account—but buying *all* of your necessities in a tourist town will add up to more than you expect.

The Checklist

Below is a checklist of things to do and things to locate before the ceremony:

- Marriage license
- Your tux, shoes, accessories
- Haircut, pedicure, etc.
- Rings
- The officiant's fee
- The rehearsal
- The gift for your bride
- Your airline tickets and passports (locate)
- Reservations (confirm)
- Cash for emergencies
- House sitter/Dog to the kennel/Mail stopped
- Arrangements for tux return

Get all these things right and you're ready for the arrival of the Big Day at long last.

CHAPTER 11

Ding Dong! Your Wedding's Here!

I t's here, it's here, it's here! Get up and rise and shine! What should you do? Should you shave, should you eat, should you be doing things that you would do on any ordinary day? First things first: Settle down before you wear yourself out with your excitement, and give yourself plenty of time to prepare for this day. This chapter contains some tips on how to have the day run smoothly, and how to make the most of your wedding day.

Nerves, Schmerves

You've planned, you've dreamed; you've saved and you've spent a lot of money on this day. It really doesn't feel so different from any other day, you're thinking as you get out of bed—until you see your wedding tux laid out on the chair, and there went your last nerve. Or is it just that you're not feeling well (because, after all, men don't get nervous about weddings)? How can you save yourself from this last-minute rush of emotions?

Ah! Cold Feet!

Feeling as though you have absolutely no business getting married? Things were going along just fine and dandy until you stood at the altar during the rehearsal and it hit you: You're a kid, for gosh sakes—a *twenty-something* kid, but a babe in arms, nonetheless. You can't be responsible for yourself, let alone a wife and a life together. What were you thinking? How is it possible that you haven't seen the writing on the wall until now?

 Fact

It's normal to be nervous on the day of any large event. Ever have to go the distance in taking an exam? Think about giving a big presentation at work. Were you sure you'd drop your props and end up jobless? Your nerves were teasing you *then*—of *course* you're nervous now!

Maybe because there is no writing on the wall, after all, or perhaps because you're reading it wrong.

Acknowledging you're a little nervous is actually a good thing. You won't be suffering from any mystery ailments, and once you realize that you are doing the right thing by marrying this incredible woman, you'll be back to your old self.

One thing's for certain: If this were not the right thing for you, you would have felt it long before today. So warm up those tootsies with a pair of woolen socks and take a deep breath. Trust the judgment that encouraged you to pop the question in the first place and realize this much: Everything's going to be A-OK.

You're So Cool

You're cool as a cucumber; you have nerves of steel. You have never buckled under the pressure of anything, so why are you feeling queasy as you prepare for your wedding? It must be the flu—or could it be that you've been *ignoring* (or, more likely, denying) the signs of wedding stress and/ or excitement?

Emotions can be tricky little things, especially for men who don't normally experience them. If this is a totally foreign feeling, you may not know what to do with it. Some tips:

♦ **Give in—a little.** Acknowledge that you're actually a little nervous. Fighting the emotion (because you're annoyed by it and/or because you perceive it as a sign of weakness) can sometimes make it worse. (On the other hand, don't give in to the anxiety so much that you're paralyzed with fright.)

- **Let it pass.** Don't dwell on the infinite realm of possibilities (i.e., maybe you're feeling nervous because you're not ready; maybe you should run away, etc.). Tell yourself that this will all pass by the end of the day.
- **Fill the time.** Don't sit around doing nothing. Get out in the world and expend some of that nervous energy.
- **If all else fails . . . all right. Go back to ignoring it.** Think about the reception and not the ceremony, if that helps; think about the honeymoon; think about your new home together.

Now's not the time to load up on the espresso, nor is it time to hit the bottle of brandy you've been saving. Ever try meditating? Sit down, close your eyes, breathe deeply, and think serene thoughts. Now stop laughing and try it again.

Just remember that you're only going to be on display for a short time; do what you have to do to get yourself through the ceremony (the most nerve-wracking part not just for grooms, but for brides, too) and realize that a great big party (and a new life) is waiting for you on the other side.

Passing Time

Some grooms find that they have almost an entire day to fill before their evening weddings. What to do? Fill the time wisely. Go to a breakfast with your dad or your brother or your best man; see a movie; take a jog or a bike ride; watch some TV; visit with out-of-town guests.

Whatever you do, don't engage in risky activities in the hours before your wedding. No one wants to hear that you wiped out on your water skis and broke your ankle, and the bride does not want you distracting attention away from her gorgeous dress with your crutches. Find something relatively safe to do today. Sorry, rock climbing with the groomsmen is out. Even though you may find it relaxing, hanging off the face of a mountain hours before your nuptials is a precarious venture. Save it for the honeymoon.

Sure, it may feel funny to sit in a movie theater and think, "I'm getting married today," but consider the alternative: Sitting at home trying to fill those hours with "normal" activities, like shaving—over and over and over again. This is not a normal day; accept it, grab someone, and find some way to pass the time.

 Essential

Evening wedding? Try to take a little nap in between your afternoon activities and preparing for the ceremony. You'll be shaking your booty all night long, so make sure you're well rested.

Just don't get so relaxed out there on the golf course or in the theater that you lose track of time (hard to do on your wedding day for most men, but very possible). Have a watch with an alarm? Set it. Have your best man set his as a backup.

The Wedding Day Schedule

While it's not possible to give a minute-by-minute description of what every groom should be doing on his wedding
day—not only because wedding times vary, but because
every groom is different—this section will give you a fairly
good idea of some areas of concern.

Risin' and Shinin'

If you have a date at the altar at ten in the morning,
you're obviously going to want to get up bright and early.
Give yourself time to have some sort of breakfast (even
though you may not feel like eating, you wouldn't want to
pass out in the middle of "I do." Not exactly the wedding of
your dreams—or your bride's); allow some time for touch-
ing base with the groomsmen and your parents.

 Fact

Give yourself a minimum of two hours to prepare yourself. You won't need every minute of that alloted time
frame, most likely, but if something doesn't turn out
right (you find that in your slightly frazzled state, you've
put toothpaste in your hair instead of gel, for example),
you'll have ample time to correct any mishaps.

If your wedding is scheduled for later in the day—late
afternoon or early evening—consider allowing yourself a
little leeway. Try *not* to be up with the birds. You're going
to need every ounce of energy you can muster today—

especially as day rolls into evening and the party kicks into high gear. You don't want to be hit with a wave of fatigue while doing the Limbo at your reception.

If all else fails and you just can't sleep in (many people have *inner* alarms that simply won't allow them to sleep past the time they normally awake), pencil in some time for a nap—or at least a little rest—for later in the day. After your round of golf or your long walk, lie down for an hour or so to recharge before you take on the task of preparing your handsome face for your wedding.

Got the Munchies?

Try not to gorge yourself prior to the wedding. Remember: You're paying top dollar for good eats later on in the day, and you don't want to arrive at the reception feeling bloated and suffering from intestinal distress due to the ten burritos you ate to stave off nerves.

 Alert

Avoid snacks that will aggravate your jitters (assuming you have a few). Caffeine, sugar, nicotine—all of these ingredients could send a trembling groom over the edge into earthquake territory. (*And* you've got the perfect setup for an upset stomach.) Take it easy on your digestive system at least until the ceremony is over.

Follow your normal diet—eat your meals when you normally would—and if you feel yourself wilting from hunger in the hours prior to the ceremony, try to snack before you step into your tux. It's all right to spill a little cocktail sauce on your white pique shirt at the reception—*after* the bulk of the professional photos have been taken. Imagine your chagrin when, years from now, you and your wife flip through your wedding album and the first thing both of you notice is the big stain on your collar.

Dressing Up

Your tux issues should have been resolved by this point, because you should have taken the time to try on your tux when you picked it up. However, on the off chance that you ignored that advice (tsk, tsk), you may discover that your cufflinks are AWOL. If you've allowed enough time for emergencies (and missing cufflinks do qualify as such on this particular day), you can send a groomsman or your sister or any able-bodied comrade over to the tux shop to take care of business.

The things you'll need to give some thought to while preparing for your wedding:

- ♦ **Cleanliness.** If you've spent the day golfing or jogging, hit the showers—please. Even if you don't detect the slightest whiff of sweat on yourself, wash up anyway. You have a long day (and night) ahead of you.
- ♦ **Grooming.** This is not the day to try out the new shaving cream or the new brand of razors—stick to the system that's been working for you. You wouldn't want to break out in an allergic rash from your new aftershave while saying your vows.

♦ **Last-minute business.** Make sure you've got everything you need for the wedding and beyond. Who has the rings? Are your bags packed? Where's the marriage license?

Getting to the Church

You'll want to allow plenty of time for traveling to the ceremony site. Each church has its own recommendation. One groom recalls that his church's advisory was for the groom and the best man to arrive one hour before the ceremony, but the groom says, "That was *way* too much time. We didn't do anything except sit in the back room and wait—and that was the only time I started to feel nervous. I would have said thirty minutes was more than enough time."

However, keep in mind that the photographer may arrive to snap a few shots of you before the ceremony; if you want a clarification as to when he'll be arriving, make sure to call and ask. It may turn out that the package you've chosen doesn't include any "extras" like these pictures of you and the best man, in which case you'll really be sitting and twiddling your thumbs until the start of the ceremony.

Again, your church will give you its own recommendations. But if the priest wants you to arrive two hours before the ceremony and you feel that's excessive, don't be afraid to raise that issue with him. It could be that ninety-nine percent of the grooms he's dealt with have made it to the church in the nick of time, and he's instituted this new policy to avoid cliff-hangers; he doesn't know that you're an absolute stickler for schedules and you would never arrive less than thirty minutes prior to the ceremony. You might save yourself a lot of annoyance by clearing up this issue before it becomes a problem.

Depending on how far you live from the church, you should always allow for extra travel time. Obviously, if you can look out your kitchen window and see the steeple, you're within walking distance and precious little will keep you from arriving on time. However, if you're traveling from one end of the city to the other—or out to the 'burbs—don't plan your travel down to the nanosecond. ("All right, I did a practice run and it took me twenty-eight minutes to get to the church; but it'll be Saturday morning and no one will be going to work, so it should take me about twenty-one and a half minutes.")

 Essential

All of your ushers should be in place at least thirty minutes prior to the ceremony to seat any early birds. (The groom's side will be to the right as you walk into the church facing the aisle; the bride's side is to the left.)

Won't you be surprised to find that everyone is on the road doing their weekend errands? It's going to take you an extra ten minutes—which means that you're going to arrive eighteen minutes before the ceremony, which isn't enough time (and this is exactly why that priest instituted his two-hour policy for grooms).

Even if you arrive in town sooner than you *need* to be there, you can always take a spin around the block; you can listen to your radio; and when the mood strikes you (and the clock dictates that you should do so), you can enter the church. Today is not the day to live by your motto: "Better late than never."

 Fact

Making arrangements for someone else to drive you to the church is a smart move, especially if you're traveling by limo from the reception to the hotel after the reception. If you can leave your car home, there's less for you to worry about.

(Candle) Lights, Camera . . .

This is it. You're sitting in the back of the church; you hear the music playing and the murmurs of the guests as they arrive. Your groomsmen occasionally poke their heads in the door to take a peek at you and make sure you're not hyperventilating, which, of course, you're not. One of them tells you that the bride's limo has arrived; it's almost time . . . you can't believe this moment has finally arrived.

Take it all in. Although you may feel downright weird because none of this seems as strange as you thought it would, realize that you're going to do this once. You won't get this day back. Do it right.

Pinch Yourself

Given to the giggles when you're nervous and/or happy? Try to quell them, if it's at all possible. Instead of whispering to your best man as your bride comes down the aisle, watch every step she takes; does she look nervous, happy, flustered? Remember: You're her rock. She wants this day to be perfect, remember—so try to avoid any behavior that would put her more on edge.

E-nun-ci-ate

When it comes time to recite your vows, take your time. There's nothing more frustrating for your guests than not being able to hear the one thing they all showed up for— the vows. Take your time, look into your bride's eyes, and say it like you mean it.

If you've written your own vows, you may know them by heart—which may encourage you to rush right through them. Don't. You've taken the time to find the exact words to express your feelings for this woman—let everyone hear what you have to say.

The Kiss

Some couples discuss the kiss at the altar prior to the ceremony; to others, it seems like the least of their worries.

Consider this: Have you ever been to a wedding where the couple gave each other the quickest little smack on the lips and you were left asking your date, "*That* was it? *That's* their kiss? Did they just take vows to be lifelong friends or husband and wife?"

Maybe not. Women notice these things more often than men do; however, your kiss will be captured on film and on video. Knowing this may only heighten your performance anxiety, but this is the moment you have to rise to the occasion and say, "The heck with the onlookers—I'm going to kiss my wife!"

Now, this doesn't mean that you should go all-out and give her the most passionate kiss you can muster—the kiss should be somewhere between the extremes. No one wants to see any groping at the altar; but the crowd wants something more satisfying than a peck on the cheek.

A good, long kiss with the appropriate amount of enthusiasm will do the trick. Practice all you want before the ceremony—this is something you want to get right.

The Big Exit

When the ceremony is over, the officiant will announce to the guests, "Ladies and Gentleman, it is my pleasure to present Mr. and Mrs. John Jones"—or something to that effect—and there will be clapping and excitement. The toughest part is over—show your extreme joy as the two of you leave the altar. Don't be afraid to cling to your new wife a little more tightly than you thought you would; don't shy away from showing your huge grin because you always imagined this day would find you feeling mature and serious. Go with the feelings you're experiencing—don't try to present some sort of wedding front. These are the pictures that are keepers.

The Reception

So you've never hosted (or attended) anything more formal than a kegger, and you're not sure how this whole reception thing is going to go. The good news is that the reception facility will be on top of the whole affair; that doesn't mean that you don't have any duties. Whether you're paying for this party or not, you're the center of attention and one of the hosts. Get ready to meet and greet.

Receiving Line

This is a line of everyone who has participated in the wedding; the guests go down the line and say hello to everyone and congratulate you and your bride. Your bride will be able to introduce you to her friends and family, and you'll do the same.

 Fact

Some churches allow for the receiving line immediately after the ceremony; some don't; and in any event, you may have guests coming to the reception who weren't able to make it to the church. Having the receiving line in your reception hall ensures that you'll be able to greet the vast majority of your guests.

Some couples opt not to have the receiving line, feeling that it's a dated idea and that the guests don't actually enjoy waiting in line—and these couples are also likely to note that a receiving line takes away from their own time at the reception. There's some truth to each of these arguments.

You should have the receiving line anyway, for these reasons:

- **You've invited these people.** You're responsible for greeting each and every one of them, and there's no easier way.
- **Any guest who doesn't want to wait in line won't.** They'll come to you later, and if they don't, it's out of your hands.
- **Your older guests will expect a receiving line and will probably think you're extremely rude if you don't have one.** You don't want to offend anyone.

No one ever died of boredom or dehydration in a receiving line, so do your best to be polite and charming to every guest who comes through. Perfect these phrases: "It's so nice to see [meet] you"; "Thank you so much for coming. It means so much to both of us"; "Go get yourself a drink before dinner." These will pretty much cover your bases.

 Essential

Keep in mind at this point that sobriety—or the appearance of it—is a virtue. Yes, it's the greatest day of your life; no, it's not a frat party. Simple piece of advice: During your reception, refrain from consuming enough alcohol to kill a horse.

Keep in mind that many reception facilities close their bars during the dinner hour, even if you've paid for an open bar. If you're just dying of thirst while you're standing in the receiving line, send your best man over to the bar to get your drink (for good measure, have him bring you some appetizers, too). Keep him on standby duty until you have greeted the last of your guests.

Your guests, meanwhile, will be ensconced in the cocktail hour after they've made it through the receiving line. They'll mosey on in to the inner sanctums of the reception hall and get themselves set up with a drink and some hors d'oeuvres. Your band or DJ will play some relaxing, light music. Folks will mingle before they find their seating cards and make their way to their tables for dinner.

Your Grand Entrance

After the guests have been seated, your wedding party will be announced by the DJ or bandleader; your parents will be announced; and lastly, you and the bride will be announced as Mr. and Mrs. Happy Couple. Standing ovation, cheers, clapping—all normal crowd reactions. You'll make your way to the head table and take your seats together.

The Speech

The best man is responsible for giving a speech before dinner. If your best man is painfully shy or horrible at speeches, he may beg to be let off the hook. If he doesn't want to give the speech, offer the opportunity to someone who wants it—another groomsman, a bridesmaid, a parent.

Tradition doesn't matter as much as sentiment in this case. A bad speech can leave a bad taste in everyone's mouth for the remainder of the evening. You and your bride will not lift your glasses and drink to yourselves; you'll simply sit there and nod appreciatively toward the toaster.

The Concerned Hosts

After you've finished your dinner, it's a nice idea for you and the bride to make your way through the tables and make sure everything is going well. If some of your guests are still waiting for their meals, one of you will need to find the banquet manager and light a fire under someone's behind.

 Fact

> A quick, "How was your dinner? Everything all right over here?" is something the banquet manager should do, but may not—and since you're the hosts, it's something you have every right (and duty) to check on.

By checking in with your guests again, you're going the extra mile—showing them that you didn't invite them just for the gifts. You care if they have a good time, if they eat, if everything is as it should be. You'll earn bonus points with many guests for this—and it's much quicker than the receiving line.

Good host that you are, you need to also keep in mind that politeness has its limits. You are not bound to sit and talk with one guest for the entire evening. Your duty is to mingle and to spend some time with your new wife. No guest should monopolize your time at your own reception. You've got a lot of guests to mingle with, and a bride who's going to want to dance with you. Excuse yourself from a guest who is chewing your ear off as politely as you can and join the party.

Wedding Traditions

There will be a lot going on during the reception—the cutting of the cake, the dancing, the throwing of the bouquet and flowers . . . keep your wits about you so that you don't miss your cues.

The Cake

The wedding cake was, in ancient times, broken over the bride's head as a symbol of fertility. You probably won't opt to follow this tradition to the letter, but most couples choose to cut the first piece together and feed each other a bite to symbolize their unity. You might want to refrain from the *other* wedding cake tradition—the one where the newlyweds smash the cake in each other's faces—unless your bride has an unusually wonderful sense of humor and won't mind you ruining her makeup and hairdo with frosting.

The Dancing

The bride's dance with her father. The groom's dance with his mother. Your first dance as a couple. The wedding party dance. So many options, so little time. You can opt to do each of these dances separately, or combine them. Have your bride start a dance with her father, and cut in midway, for example. Some brides dig the splendor of all of the dance numbers, but if you think this is going to go on for way too long, or you don't particularly want to be out on that huge dance floor with your mom for five long minutes, put on your thinking cap and get creative.

Choose appropriate music for this occasion. If you like a song and you think you might want it for your first dance with your bride, take the time to actually listen to the lyrics. Is it a love song, or is it a song about breaking up? Is it a song about coming together after being apart, or does the actual theme deal with death? Don't count on your DJ or band leader to counsel you here; do your homework and weed out the less suitable songs before one of your guests points out that you just symbolized your union by dancing to a song about someone's dead pet.

The Garter and the Bouquet

Once a staple at receptions, the whole tossing of the garter and the bouquet is falling by the wayside in many areas. If you opt to continue the tradition of reaching way up under your bride's dress in order to find the blue silk garter, do it as tastefully as possible, while having a sense of humor. Once you find it, you'll throw it into a crowd of the single men in attendance. The guy who snags it will be front and center in a moment . . .

The bride's throwing of the bouquet is supposed to predict marriage for the lucky girl who catches it. This same girl is then subjected to having the garter placed on her leg by the recipient of the garter. The higher he goes with it, the better your luck as newlyweds, or so the story goes.

Keep this under control. If your female guest is obviously embarrassed by the whole thing, have a heart and don't insist that the garter go higher and higher up her leg. You want everyone to have pleasant memories of this evening, after all.

Essential

Don't cross over into extremely raunchy territory, especially if most of your guests are from the older generation. They may not find it funny when you actually crawl under the dress and stay there.

The Getaway

No doubt, some of your buddies will decorate your car with streamers and shaving cream and hopefully nothing that's more distasteful. Centuries ago, guests threw old shoes at the newlyweds' carriage for luck; this translated into the tradition of tying old shoes onto the back of a car; from there, we arrive at today's tradition of trashing the getaway car. Hey, they're just wishing you luck and hiding in the bushes laughing at your consternation of having to clean the car off before you can actually drive it. Only true friends would do that for you.

Your New Mrs.

Keep in mind, there are three kinds of brides out there: Those who keep it together throughout the engagement and completely lose it on the wedding day; those who are a mess until they walk through the doors of the church—and then miraculously regain their composure; and those who are a little unbearable from the time they start planning the wedding till the time life settles into some kind of routine after the marriage.

(There is a fourth, rare bride type—the one who is completely normal during her engagement and has a great time at the wedding. If this is your girl, acknowledge how amazing she is.)

So if your bride does not appear to be enjoying herself on your wedding day, don't attribute it to anything other than nerves. Yes, she loves you; yes, she's glad she married you; and yes, she will return to acting like herself in no time.

CHAPTER 12

The Happily Ever After Part

The ceremony was perfect; the reception went off without a hitch; the honeymoon was paradise; now you're back home and you've got some work to do. There's the matter of writing all of those thank-you notes; there's the budget to discuss; one of you may be moving in to the other's home. Being a great partner isn't hard—and you've already come so far, there's no doubt that you can go the extra mile.

Thank You, Thank You

You feel as though you've been living life in the spotlight, and now that the wedding's over, it's over. No more worrying about the details, just thinking back and remembering how great the day was. Hang on. You're not *quite* ready to write the wedding off until you've written your thank-you notes. Get your pen ready, Mister.

The Parade of Gifts

Upon returning from the honeymoon (or from the wedding if you're delaying the honeymoon for a while), you and the bride will dig into a seemingly never-ending mountain of wedding gifts. Before you do, make sure you're set up to record each gift. You should know who gave you what, because you can't properly thank someone if you're completely clueless as to what they gave you—or if they gave you anything at all.

 Essential

A gift recorder doesn't have to be a fancy, store-bought item. Take a sheet of paper and make two columns: Name and Gift—and don't lose this list!

"She'll Write All the Notes"

No, she won't. Time was, the bride was held responsible for sending the perfect note of gratitude to each and every wedding guest. Your wife simply cannot complete the tasks of the average 1950s housewife. She has a full-time job of her own, plus the housework. In addition, you're a Man of the New Millennium—and as such, you're expected to help out.

Look at it this way—is it really fair to expect your wife to write 200 letters of appreciation while you flat-out refuse to do it? No, not really.

Divide the duties any way that seems feasible to both of you. Perhaps you'd feel most comfortable writing to your own friends and members of your family. Or maybe you'd like to switch lists and have her address your side of the guest list while she sends notes to your relations.

Expressing Your Gratitude

Whatever your personal feelings for a particular guest, if he or she brought you a gift, you must send a thank you. Even if you absolutely hate the gift, even if you cannot for the life of you understand how someone looked at this hideous lamp and decided you would love it, even if you think it's a re-gift, you have to send the thank you.

Many new grooms are faced with the realization that they have never been forced to write a note of thanks. No matter. It's easy enough. A few simple guidelines:

- **Get the names right.** There's nothing more offensive to a gift giver than being addressed by the wrong name. Check and double-check names (and spellings) if you're unsure.
- **Keep it brief.** No one expects a three-page letter from a newlywed.

◆ **Make mention of the gift.** The giver wants to know that you actually made note of the gift and that you know what you're thanking them for. An all-purpose line like "Thank you for your wedding gift" is very vague and suspicious—as though you have no idea what this person gave you.

 Fact

Even if this is the worst gift you've received over the course of your lifetime and assuming that you've accepted the fact that you absolutely have to thank the giver, be as sincere as you can when writing your note of thanks. (In other words, don't try to craft an ambiguous—and sarcastic—communiqué.)

You *still* haven't the slightest idea where to start? Let's say your Aunt Peg sent you a check for your wedding. You need to send her a thank-you note, and you should do it within the month. If you wait any longer, Peg will wonder if her check got lost in the mail—and when she checks her bank statement and realizes you've already cashed it, she's going to be awfully miffed at your bad manners.

Since Peg sent you money, you're going to thank her and tell her what you plan to do with that money:

Dear Aunt Peg,

Thank you so much for the wedding gift. We've just started looking at houses and plan to use the money toward a down payment.

We're sorry that you couldn't make it to the wedding, but we appreciate your thoughtfulness.

Thanks again.

Love,

Joe and Jojo

Note how the actual monetary amount doesn't make its way into the letter—Aunt Peg might have given you $25, or maybe she sent you $500. It doesn't matter. Etiquette states that you leave the dollar amount out of the thank-you letter.

Now, what if Aunt Peg came to the wedding and gave you the aforementioned hideous lamp?

Dear Aunt Peg,

Thank you very much for the lamp. It's just what we needed for our apartment. The colors in the lampshade are so vivid that it matches everything.

We were so glad you could come to the wedding. It meant a lot to both of us that you were there to share our special day.

Thanks again.

Love,

Joe and Jojo

Note that nothing in this letter is an actual lie.

The main idea you want to get across is that you are appreciative of the specific gift that this person gave you, and that you were happy they were at your wedding. It's not difficult; you'll get the hang of it and find yourself adding little niceties like, "Hope to see you soon!" and "Give us a call next time you're in town!" Easy breezy.

The Forgotten

Once in a while, a gift-giver's name will get lost or you'll simply forget to send a thank-you note. If the slighted person happens to be a relative, you'll probably hear about it through the grapevine (read: your mom). As soon as you hear the rumblings that you've forgotten to thank someone, get on the stick and get that note out ASAP.

 Alert

You have thirty days to get a thank-you note to a gift giver. Don't put the entire task off for three weeks and then try to work your way through a mound of stationery. Writing ten or fifteen notes a night will make the task much more manageable.

Sure, you might feel funny sending a thank-you note to someone who's obviously peeved at you for not sending one, but the alternative is that you're thought of—and spoken of—as a crass nincompoop. (And if it doesn't matter to you, it does matter to someone else—yes, your mom—so just do it.)

If you have no idea at this point what this person has given you, you have no other choice but to use vague language, which is a no-no in most cases. This is the better of two bad choices. It's better to send a note that's a little unclear on the facts than to ignore the giver. That's just wrong.

What's Her Name?

The subject of the bride's surname is usually less of an issue for the newlyweds and more of a predicament for those outside your immediate circle of family and friends—folks who are caught off guard by a bride's decision to keep her maiden name and who don't hide their disapproval well.

If you're the one who's unhappy with her decision, cut her some slack. Wouldn't it seem strange to you if you were the one who was expected to suddenly take on a new identity? Tradition aside, it doesn't really matter which name your wife goes by—she's still your partner for life.

Why?

If you were thinking that your new wife would come around and see the wisdom of taking your name after the wedding—and she hasn't—you may be wondering what the big deal is. It's just a name, after all, and women have taken their husbands' names for years.

Consider these points:

- Today's women often establish themselves in the business world using their maiden name and are reluctant to throw clients and customers into any sort of confusion.
- The changing of the wife's name seemed much more appropriate when women stayed at home and couldn't make a move—financially or otherwise—without their husband's assistance.
- With the whole gender-equality issue coming to the forefront in the past few decades, women are really questioning the fairness of the expectation to change their names.

 Essential

A bride's decision to keep her maiden name should never be interpreted as a disrespectful move, or as a sign that she doesn't think much of the groom's family.

Slow Compromise

Still not convinced that her refusal to take your name is not a reflection of her feelings for you? Some brides take their time with the name-changing process. One bride recalls her struggle with the name issue: "I kept my maiden name because as far as I was concerned, it was silly to take a new name. I had been working for years; all my contacts knew me by my maiden name, and I had experienced the confusion of name changes in the office first-hand.

"Well, my husband's family wasn't happy at all, and they weren't shy about letting me know it. About six months after we got married, I started thinking about tacking my married name onto my maiden name, but it took me much longer because my in-laws made it such a huge deal. I didn't want it to seem like I was giving in to them, because in the end, it was my decision, even though my husband kept trying to tell me that his family should be allowed to comment. I disagreed then, and I disagree now. No one was asking their son to alter *his* name in any way, after all."

 Alert

If you're married to a particularly strong-willed woman, pushing her on the issue of changing her name to yours may result in a stonewall response. Better to let her decide on her own, and in her own time.

So here the bride has addressed two issues: First, that a combination of the two names is sometimes a suitable alternative to the traditional changing of her surname; and secondly, that the decision has to be hers, unless she asks for input.

Some grooms choose to take on a hyphenated version of their surname and their bride's. When children come along (if they do), they'll have the identity of both parents, which is something children of past generations never had. Meanwhile, you and the bride have made an equal concession—and gained an equal share—in the name game.

Movin' In

If you and your bride had been cohabitating for years, then you won't have to address the obvious living issues that face separate dwellers. If your bride is just moving her boxes into your place this very moment, you're going to have an adjustment period.

"Hey, That's My Drawer!"

You had to know that your wife expects to have some space of her own—so try not to pull any last-minute space issues out of thin air. She has to have someplace to put her clothes; she needs to keep her toiletries in the bathroom; and yes, she's probably even going to expect to bring some books and knick-knacks.

This may be a sensitive issue if you're very particular about where things should be, and especially if you've been living on your own for a decade. It's going to take some getting used to, but she's here now, and you can't keep every inch of storage and display space for your own. Share and share alike.

Baring It All

Funny thing happens when people move in together—they see each other at their absolute worst moments. If you're moving into your bride's apartment and you never really noticed how gross her shower is, or that she uses some kind of weird cream on her armpits to reduce perspiration . . . you're feeling taken right now. Would you have married a woman with such issues had you known? Who can say for sure?

Although she could say the same thing about you and the way you cut your toenails over the toilet, always managing to leave a sharp piece on the floor that she always ends up stepping on.

 Essential

The best way to deal with the personal grossness that affects every human being? Have a sense of humor—to a point. If the issue is a real matter of hygiene—the shower curtain is covered in some kind of . . . *something*, for example—a discussion is in order.

Divide and Conquer the Household

You both work full-time. You're both too exhausted to take on the added headache of keeping house. What's a married couple to do? Get everything out in the open, for starters. Listen to what she expects from you; tell her what you're expecting from her. If you both end up rolling on the floor laughing (because you've just told her that you expect *her* to keep the place spotless, and she's just said that she thought you knew how to fix things), you're going to need to work a few things out.

Who's Doing What?

There are bound to be some things that are either difficult (you wouldn't expect your five-foot wife to clean the shelves in the garage that are at your arm's reach) or distasteful to one or both of you. Say, for example, that you absolutely cannot mop the kitchen floor without making a huge mess. At the same time, your wife has the whole mopping thing down to a science, but she despises cleaning the bathroom—a chore that you actually don't mind tackling. The solution is obvious, but only if you open the lines of communication, which neither of you may do if you're trying to keep the peace or the status quo.

If it's really important to one (or each) of you to keep the house running like clockwork, make a schedule of which chores are done and when. Maybe you don't want to spend your Saturday scrubbing the toilet bowl—but you wouldn't mind doing it during the week. Knowing that it's going to be done on a regular basis (whether it's Wednesday or the weekend) should be enough for a partner who's a little obsessive about scheduling.

Know when obsession is crossing the line, though. You're newlyweds and you only have a short time to be newlyweds. If fun presents itself, let the floors go one more day without a scrubbing.

Maintenance

Once you buy a home, the issue of maintenance pops up—every weekend for the rest of your lives, until you realize the wisdom of your parents' generation, living in maintenance-free neighborhoods. But that's decades down the road. Right now, you and your bride are the cleanup and repair crew dedicated to keeping your home in ship-shape condition.

Everyone has to do some chores that are distasteful or dull or monotonous—but make sure that one of you isn't stuck doing the worst jobs all the time, especially if you're both working an equal amount of time outside of the home. If your wife wants to mow the lawn one gorgeous weekend while *you* stay inside and do the dusting, make the trade. You'll both be happier for it.

 Fact

You may be surprised to realize what you're capable of. Many home-improvement stores have free how-to clinics for the most common household problems and projects, as well.

Another issue that may pop up is whether you're a home-repair expert—and/or whether your new wife expects you to be one. Girls who grow up in households headed by handymen expect an awful lot from their new husbands. Your wife may think you know how to rewire a circuit and lay tile—because that's what husbands do on the weekend, as far as she's concerned. If you find yourself on the losing end of a long list of household projects she has laid out for you and you wouldn't even know where to begin with any of them, don't explode.

Here's a perfect opportunity for you, if you're of the mind-set to accept it. You can either ask your new father-in-law for help (and really get to know him in the process), or you can dig in to some do-it-yourself books.

Of course, no one is saying that you have to learn these things—and no one's saying you have to tackle these projects on your own. If you and/or your wife can learn a thing or two about repairs, though, you'll save yourselves a bundle in the long run.

Alert

Calling a plumber for a leaky sink is like taking your car to the mechanic: There are some honest guys out there, and some guys who'll rob you blind—and if you don't know the first thing about the problem at hand, you're setting yourself up for a big loss.

The Budget

Household Budgeting. Sounds like something your mom did, just before she baked a cake from scratch, right? Well, you and your bride may opt for the store-bought confections, but no one can draw up a budget for yourselves better than the two of you can. And since you may be overwhelmed with all the wedding moola you've received as gifts, now's a good time to get down to the business of deciding where that money would be best spent—before it disappears.

One word of advice before you start: Give yourselves a block of time some night or weekend when you're not pressed by ten other engagements. This is a duty that requires careful consideration on both of your parts.

The Groundwork

Money, money, money. It causes happiness, it provokes craziness, and it often leads to the biggest arguments in any given marriage. Since the last thing you want is for this budgeting session to devolve into The Silent Treatment (that would be decidedly counterproductive), it's important that each of you approach this meeting seriously and open-mindedly—and that you agree from the beginning not to go to war over any one budgeting issue.

 Fact

Successfully hammering out a financial plan sometimes takes weeks or months, so if there's a real sticking point somewhere along the line, realize that this is not unusual—but you will need to come to terms on the issue (hopefully sooner rather than later).

From the get-go, you'll need to identify yourselves. Since, at this point, you know each other intimately, you'll be identifying your spending habits. Are you a saver or a spender? Is your wife frugal or free with cash? Be honest with your assessment of yourself and give each other the opportunity to disagree with the self-evaluations.

If, for example, your wife identifies herself as extremely thrifty, but she's sitting across the table from you wearing a blouse that cost roughly the same amount as your monthly rent, you might want to bring up the discrepancy—gently. But be prepared to hear from her that your tennis shoes were approximately the same price as your car payment.

The important thing here is to get the conversation started. Ignoring the fact that one of you is spending every last penny on frivolous purchases will only lead to bigger problems down the road. Many couples choose to ignore their hemorrhagic cash flow problems rather than fight over them. These are often the same couples that are up to their ears in debt and have scary credit ratings.

You Want to Eat This Month?

If both of you are new to the budgeting scene, you'll want to address the basics first. Take both of your pay-checks and total your take-home pay for the month. There's your base number.

Next, make a list of your monthly expenditures: car payments; your rent or mortgage; student (or other) loan payments; food; credit cards; utilities (heat, electricity, phone, water). Your rent is set in stone, as are your other loans—for now. See if there's any way to cut back on your other expenses. Do you eat out every single night? Dining at home is much cheaper.

Are both of you in the habit of charging everything, resulting in sky-high credit card bills? Try carrying cash for a week and using the cards only for emergencies—you may find it's much harder for you to fork over actual money, and you might also find yourself realizing just how much (read: too much) you've been paying for things when you're forced to actually think about its price.

You might feel like your father when you go about trying to reduce your electric bill by turning lights off when you leave a room—but you're on to your father's secret. He decided a long time ago to keep his money instead of giving it to the electric company out of the goodness of his heart. When you're ready to follow in these footsteps, look into the further possibilities of not giving money away to the other utility companies. Turn the water off when you're brushing your teeth. Turn the heat down at night and when you leave the house and when you're away for the weekend. Maybe you don't need to be paying for call waiting when neither of you is ever home to use the phone anyway.

Big Expenses

You may be wondering what the big deal is. You've both been living on your own, and moving in together is going to save you a lot of money right off the bat. That's great.

What are you going to do with that money? Will you invest it, buy a house, pay off outstanding loans, decorate your new home?

What are you saving for, you ask? What good is money that's off limits?

Two schools of thought: Save for a purchase (you want to pay cash for your next car, for example, or you want to establish a savings fund for your child's education, or you may want to start a business in a year or two), or save for emergencies.

Yeah, yeah. You have credit and credit will always see you through. Stop right there. Think about a worst-case scenario down the road: You lose your job. Your wife is injured and is forced to stop working. You have kids, a mortgage, two car payments, credit card bills, and various other expenditures (you know, like food and heat). Depressing? Yes, it is. (Apologies.) However, you could possible find yourself in a very difficult financial situation someday—and wouldn't it be nice to know that you have six months of living expenditures socked away?

 Essential

Keep in mind that although you may be tempted to drop a big wad of cash on new purchases for your home, this is a never-ending process. You'll never be finished. It's a good idea to establish a habit of saving as soon as you're able to squirrel a little something away each month.

The hard reality of life is that your situation, as great as it is right now, can turn on a dime—and it's always best to be prepared.

Husband of the Year

How long will it be before your house and marriage are running like a well-oiled machine and you don't need to talk about the budget and the chores and the (gasp!) gross shower curtain? That depends on you, in part.

Don't Be Afraid of Problems

Establishing a life with a life partner isn't all fun and games. Unfortunately, no matter how hard you try to avoid life's little annoyances, they'll always be there. Some couples simply don't like to argue, so they end up ignoring issues (like budgeting, like home projects) until someone gets so irritated that the initial, smallish problem is blown way out of proportion—and at that point, the hope of calmly resolving the issue is all but lost.

 Fact

A partner who isn't willing to pick up the slack once in a while will sometimes drive the other partner to keep score (as in, "Well, if you aren't going to help *me*, why should I help *you*?").

Communicate with each other in a respectful manner before problems reach a boiling point.

Help Out

Even if it's her turn to scrub the grout, if she's overloaded with work this week or she's got the flu . . . why not tackle the chore for her? This is just the impetus many couples need in order to establish the essential give-and-take that make successful relationships thrive.

Little things really do tip the scales in a marriage, for better or for worse. If you make every effort to go out of your way for her—to be considerate, to help her when she needs it, to compliment her appearance when she's wearing nothing special . . . you'll be light years ahead of many of your contemporaries. Start clearing a space on your mantel for the Husband Hall of Fame plaque. You're earning it every day.

Invitations

Years ago, deciding on the invitation wording was a simple task. The bride's parents paid for the whole wedding, and so there was no question about who was doing the inviting. Now, of course, couples often pay for their own weddings, and/or both sets of parents chip in for the expense. Add stepparents to the mix, and you might just be thinking about forgetting the whole invitation thing and relying on word of mouth. Plenty of people will show up when they hear about it on the street, right?

The Couple as Hosts

If you and your bride are the hosts, your invitation can read something like this:

"Carol Ann Smith and John Jones cordially invite you to attend the celebration of their marriage . . . "

Pertinent information concerning the date and time, as well as the reception information follows, of course.

Both Sets of Parents

If everyone's involved here, you can go with a traditional-sounding invitation:

"Mr. and Mrs. Albert Smith
and
Mr. and Mrs. Harold Jones
cordially invite you to attend the marriage of their children,
Carol Ann
and
John . . . "

Bride's Divorced Parents as Hosts

"Mrs. Lucille Smith (bride's mother)
and
Mr. Albert Smith (bride's father)

request the honor of your presence at the marriage

of their daughter,

Carol Ann,

to

Mr. John Jones . . . "

Stepparents

Just take things to the next logical step when including step-parents. The bride's family is listed first, and her mother is mentioned before her father:

"Lucille Smith (bride's mother, divorced, not remarried)

and

Albert and Kathleen Smith (bride's

father, divorced, remarried)

together with

Helen and Robert Nelson (groom's

mother, divorced, remarried)

and

Ellen and Harold Jones (groom's

father, divorced, remarried)

request the honor of your presence at

the marriage of their children,

Carol Ann

and

John . . . "

Invitation Pointers

- Use Mr. and Mrs. where appropriate on the invitation itself.
- Use full names (even though everyone calls you Jack, John should be written on the invitation—assuming your real name is John, of course).
- No abbreviations. None. Even the year is spelled out.
- When addressing the envelopes, *always* use appropriate titles: Mr., Mrs., Dr., etc.

Registry Guide

Assuming you're going to accompany your bride to the big department store (or the small boutique) to register for gifts, choose wisely. You'll need the pots and pans more than that really cool massaging apparatus.

These are the absolute bare essentials. Any store that has a registry will hand you a preprinted sheet on which you can simply check off the items you'd like and the quantities of each. Don't skip any of these items in favor of less useful items. You get this one chance to have others stock your home for you.

Registry Essentials

- Dishes
- Stemware (Wine glasses, water goblets, champagne flutes. Shotglasses are not a staple item.)
- Barware (Pilsner glasses, hefty beer mugs, martini glasses, rocks glasses, etc.)
- Everyday glasses
- Flatware (Choose stainless steel for everyday use.)
- Formal flatware (Silver for entertaining.)

These are the basics, and depending on your love of or disdain for entertaining, you should think about sets of eight to twelve for each of these pieces. In addition, there are some extras for the table:

- Serving dishes
- Platters
- Soup tureen
- Gravy boat
- Chafing dish
- Salt and pepper shakers

Cookware/Ovenware

The bare minimum:

- Skillet (Preferably of the nonstick variety and preferably something of quality. Electric or stovetop.)
- Tea kettle
- Pots (You'll need varying sizes here, for convenience. A large stockpot is great for lobsters; a small saucepan is perfect for boiling peas; and a medium pot is just right for pasta.)
- Broiling pan
- Roasting pan
- Oven- and microwave-safe ceramic cookware

Kitchen Items

The things you can't be without:

- Coffeemaker (for company if not for you)
- Toaster
- Mixer
- Blender and mixing bowls
- Knives
- Food processor
- Microwave
- Utensils: ladle, can opener, bottle opener, mixing spoons, measuring cups, pizza cutter, corkscrew, colander, spatulas, meat thermometer

♦ Kitchen linens: oven mitts, pot holders, dishtowels, napkins, placemats

Linens: Bath

♦ Washcloths
♦ Towels
♦ Handtowels (Think six to eight for each—and for each bathroom.)
♦ Shower curtain
♦ Bathmat

Linens: Bed

♦ Comforter
♦ Blanket
♦ Duvet cover
♦ Sheets (At least three sets: flat and fitted.)
♦ Pillow cases and shams

Tipping Guide

Remember: European hotels and restaurants and all-inclusive resorts usually have the gratuity added in to the bill. Don't double-tip . . . unless you feel extremely free with your money. Back here in the States, the guidelines for filling those outstretched hands are as follows:

- **Waiters/waitresses:** 15 to 20 percent of the dinner bill, depending on the service.
- **Coatcheck:** A dollar or two a couple.
- **Restroom attendants:** Fifty cents to $1.
- **Bartenders:** A buck a round, if it's just you and your wife ordering drinks.
- **Wine stewards:** 15 to 20 percent of the wine bill.
- **Buffet servers:** A dollar or two per person if the service has been good.
- **Room service:** Check the bill when you sign for your order—often, the gratuity will be added to the bill. Otherwise, 15 to 20 percent of the total.
- **Bellboys:** $1 a bag; $1 for opening the room; $5 for sending him on an errand. (Adjust this rate to the city. In New York or San Francisco, up the tip a bit.)
- **Chambermaids:** A dollar or two a night.
- **Concierge:** $5 to $10 for booking reservations or securing theater tickets.
- **Valet:** $2 to $3.
- **Maitre'd:** $20 to $100, depending on the restaurant, depending on how badly you want to eat there, and depending on how long you want to wait for a table.
- **Doorman:** $1 to $2 for hailing a cab; $2 to $5 for helping with bags.

If you're headed off on a cruise, you're entering an entirely different tipping environment—the good news is that each cruise line will provide you with tipping guidelines.

Remember: Tipping is always voluntary—but if someone really goes out of their way for you and your bride on your honeymoon, make sure you reward them appropriately.

Index

Made in the USA
San Bernardino, CA
20 January 2018